# GOD IS A DIVORCÉ TOO!

## A MESSAGE OF *Hope,* *Healing,* AND *Forgiveness*

### SHERMAN NOBLES

TATE PUBLISHING, LLC

ISBN: 1-9331481-8-7

# ENDORSEMENTS

Freedom is the central message; courage with practice-oriented scholarship profiles the author.

The result: 'A more excellent way' to view and deal with this difficult subject of divorce.

**Dr. Carle M. Hunt**, D.B.A., M.B.A., B.S., B.A.

Professor, School of Education, Regent University, VA


This is a compelling book which helps pastors and laity alike understand how the worldview of culture has negatively influenced how the church handles and wounds those struggling with divorce. It is a seminal work for study and policy development in how we can better help those marginalized by divorce. Brilliant!

**Reverend Dr. Sandra J. Taulbee**, D.M.H., M.Div., M.Ed.

Interim Head of Staff, Central Presbyterian Church,

Huntington, NY


The core message of the New Testament is that salvation is received by grace through faith. But that liberating concept is difficult to grasp for people who have been taught that the only way to please God is through man's religious systems. In his groundbreaking book, *God is a Divorce' Too!*, Sherman Nobles skillfully and mercifully slaughters one of religion's sacred cows, the issue of Christians and divorce.

Arguing from a firm position of New Testament grace, Sherman tackles such thorny theological questions as, "Is divorce a sin?", "Is marriage a sacrament?", "Is marriage indissoluble?", and "Are there morally-acceptable reasons for divorce?" Through the entire book, Sherman defends the divine ideal of marriage, while bringing freedom and comfort to those who have suffered the devastation of divorce.

For too long, the church has cast out wounded people who have suffered the shipwreck of divorce! Through this important book, I pray that ministers and denominations will prayerfully consider their position on marriage and divorce from a balanced, New Testament perspective of forgiveness and grace—so that the Church, on this crucial issue, may truly reflect the love of Jesus Christ.

**Craig von Buseck**, M.A. in Religious Journalism
Programming Director of CBN.com and Ordained Minister
Author of *Seven Keys to Hearing God's Voice*

This book is far more than the title discloses. While I began reading expecting a book focusing on issues of divorce and remarriage, to my delight I discovered a wealth of spiritual insight and wisdom on many areas of life including dating, marriage, family, and more! I want to use this book to share with my teenagers the biblical wisdom shared on these issues they are dealing with now. This book will delight you with fresh insights and drive you to the scriptures, and hopefully, to Jesus Himself as well. I highly recommend this for all those who are lovers of God.

**Liz Adleta**, Executive Director,
Global Christian Network, Inc., Virginia Beach, VA

The topic of divorce is as emotionally painful as it is theologically complex in the church. It is an unfortunate truth that many talented and anointed Christians, because of man-made moral and ethical restrictions on divorcées, live a life less than what God intended for them. Yet, we can draw insight from William Shakespeare who once wrote, "There is a tide in the affairs of men." I believe Shakespeare was expressing his observation of the changing tides of history and if embraced, its inevitable impact on human kind. In the book *God is a Divorcé Too!*, the author masterfully captures the essence of God's greatest desire and that is to forgive us, despite our faults.

In Genesis, God's first aspect of proclaiming his blessing on mankind was a command to be "fruitful and multiply," in essence to increase and expand. This book on divorce in the church is a relevant literary and theological work that reflects a tide destined to change the traditional perspective of many theological thinkers. The author offers a fresh, yet biblically sound perspective that will set thousands of divorcées free from bondage, thus bringing Kingdom increase as God commanded in the book of Genesis.

Like me, I believe at the end of this book, you will conclude that this work is timely and relevant. I am grateful to have had the honor and privilege of reviewing and endorsing this revolutionary work on the topic of divorce.

**Pastor Rupert H. George**, B.S. in Psychology and Sociology
Bethel Christian Fellowship, Virginia Beach, VA
Pentecostal Holiness (IPHC)


Rather than relying on the pronouncements of church tradition or on any examples of conventional wisdom, Nobles simply allows Scripture to explain Scripture. You may not agree with everything this author sets forth. Yet you cannot help but be challenged by his reasoned approach. If "speaking the truth in love" be a biblical mandate, Sherman Nobles has obeyed admirably.

**Charles J. Dunleavy Jr.**, A.B., B.Th.
Ordained Minister with the Church of Christ


I welcome this significant discussion of a matter of extreme pain and misunderstanding in the Christian community. Sherman Nobles has endeavored to deal thoroughly with all of the issues associated with divorce, particularly the biblical and ecclesial matters. As an Old Testament student, I am pleased that someone has illuminated the divine experience of divorce, particularly in light of the Old Testament prophetic teachings of Jeremiah and especially Hosea.

Knowing that God identifies with and shares this same experience places an entirely different perspective even on the biblical text that states, "I [i.e. God] hate divorce" (Malachi 2:16). Those who seek scriptural guidance and have interest in seeing that God's mercy is fully applied to those who have experienced loss and rejection, will find this a most helpful work.

**Dr. Randall J. Pannell**, Ph.D., M.Div., B.A.
Associate Professor of Hebrew and Old Testament
Associate Dean for Academics
School of Divinity, Regent University, VA

In a world that is greatly confused about God's relationship with the divorcée, Nobles has allowed the Holy Spirit to direct him down a path that has been considered taboo in the Christian and religious world. After reading _God is a Divorcé Too_! I have a deeper understanding of the unconditional love and acceptance of God the Father for those who are hurting from the effects of divorce. I say to the person who is struggling or has struggled with the bondage of divorce, 'Read this book!' for it will be used by the Holy Spirit to free you from the misunderstandings and misinterpretations of Scriptures that have kept you from seeing God as "Abba" Father.

**Associate Pastor Demetrius Boucher**, M.A. in Divinity
Sounder's Road Nazarene Church, Hampton, VA


Finally, a teaching that holds the guilty party accountable, and frees and empowers the victim!

**Pastor John Dupont**, B.A., Celebration Church,Virginia Beach, VA


Insightful, Perplexing, Thought-provoking --- A Compelling Page-turner!

**Professor Margaret Gums**, M.A. in Communications


As a divorcée, I found this book refreshing, packed full of bondage breaking facts. As a prayer counselor, it has helped tremendously in my ministry to hurting people with broken relationships.

**Dolores Chappell**, Chesapeake, VA
Messianic Jew and Prayer Counselor


This book has helped me so much and I know many people that need to read it. I knew deep in my heart that I was free to remarry, although that is not what is taught in my denomination. Your book also revealed some issues that I needed to deal with, helping heal the relationship between my ex-husband and I, so that we can at least be friends for the kid's sake.

**Pastor Carmen Everett**, Chesapeake, VA
Nehemiah Restoration Worship Ministries, Chesapeake, VA

# TESTIMONIES

**Gail** said, "Remarkable thing to me is...you've not been through a divorce, yet you seem to completely identify with the pain and the despair associated with divorce. It is a horrible experience and to have it happen once or twice in your life will destroy your trust. With information like yours, people ravaged by divorce may have the heart to try to trust one more time. Most of them can't even trust God. So learning to trust Him would be a HUGE step forward.

**Rebecca**, a 21-year-old woman, read *God is a Divorcé Too!* the weekend that she left her husband after having been married for less than a year. She said, "What I read helped free me from the condemnation that others had put me under by implying that I was at fault in some way for my husband's abusive acts against me. It inspired me to seek God more because of the seriousness of the decision that I have to make concerning my marriage. It also freed me from the fear that if we divorce that I could never again marry with God's blessing. I realized that God is on my side and not against me, and I am free to divorce my husband if needed. Surprisingly, understanding these things frees me to wait on God. God has my best at heart, so I need to seek His will concerning my situation. I don't need to be anxious about this, but I need to wait on God to work things out, however He does that. He will show me the way." Thankfully, they have worked things out and are now back together.

**Gregg**, 40, a pastor and teacher, was in the middle of divorce proceedings (against his will and desires) when he read the manuscript. He said, "While I was reading the manuscript, I fell asleep about half way through (not because it was boring, but because I was physically exhausted). When I awoke, I felt freer, like something had been lifted off of my shoulders. I can't explain it, because I can't say that I believe everything you wrote, although it makes sense and I can't argue with your logic. I've been taught the traditional doctrine so long, that it's hard to accept what you've written, but I can't find anything specific to disagree with either. But I do know that I feel freer since having read your book."

**Jodie** previewed an early version of the manuscript. At the time she had no idea that her husband would leave her within the next few months for another woman. A couple of days after he left, I spoke with her asking how she was doing. After a few comments concerning her emotional well being, she made the following unsolicited comments concerning the manuscript. "Your book helped prepare me to handle the current problems between my husband and I. Because of what I learned from your book, I can continue to go to church and seek the Lord without feeling guilty, or like there is something wrong with me. I don't fear having a big "A" (Adulterer) or "D" (Divorcée) tattooed on my forehead because of my husband's bad decisions. I am also not overly anxious about my situation and trying to MAKE things work out, because regardless of what happens to my marriage, I can continue to love and seek God. I believe that God will help me through whatever is to come–reconciliation or divorce." Thankfully, they too have reunited.

# DEDICATION

To those who have been divorced, may you forgive us, the church, for condemning and rejecting you when you needed us most! May God use this book to liberate you from false religious bondage, comfort you, and give you hope!

To Chantal, the wife of my youth, my best friend, and partner in life! You inspire me to be a better man, father, and friend.

To my children, may what is written herein help you establish healthy, strong, and enduring marriages filled with the love of God!

To pastors, may this book equip you to impart the forgiveness, healing, and hope that are found in the Gospel for the divorcée!

# ACKNOWLEDGEMENTS

*Foremost, I thank God.* I have experienced many answers to prayer for wisdom, understanding, insight, provision, and resources. I have often felt His inspiration and encouragement, especially through His people, the Body of Christ. Thank you, Father.

*Chantal,* my wife, thank you for supporting me in this project, and especially for listening to hours of seemingly endless conversation concerning this book. Thank you for your faithful love, trust, and respect.

*Patricia Baron,* my mother-in-law, thank you for your support personally and in helping publish this book.

*Mom and Dad,* thank you for your love and support. Thank you for doing your best in hard times, for not allowing your divorce to make you bitter or resentful, and for always encouraging me in the Lord.

*Tom Tierney,* thank you very much for the sample cover designs that you put together for me when I first started writing this book. They were a great encouragement and a constant source of inspiration.

*Jack Doussard,* thank you for reminding me of King David's relationship with Michal, his first wife, an important biblical example of a man putting away (abandoning) his wife, causing her to commit adultery.

*Tate Publishing*, thank you for being brave enough to publish such a controversial title and for endorsing its message.

A very special thanks is due those who were willing to brave the treacherous waters of tradition and endorse this work. Thank you! I also appreciate very much the many other friends, pastors, and professors who have taken of their time to critique this work and offer constructive criticism. They have helped make this a much better book. Thank you Lisa Wentland, Matt Eichman, Don McNeely, Pastor Roger Stephens, Pastor Ben Purdum, and Pastor Abel Laureless.

# BIBLICAL TRANSLATIONS

| | |
|---|---|
| AEM | The Holy Bible from Ancient Eastern Manuscripts |
| CEV | Contemporary English Version |
| KJV | King James Version |
| NAB | New American Bible |
| NCV | New Century Version |
| NIV | New International Version |
| NKJV | New King James Version |
| NLT | New Living Translation |
| NRSV | New Revised Standard Version |

# MISHNAIC AND TALMUDIC REFERENCES

Tractates will not be abbreviated; however, to distinguish tractates with the same name in the Mishnah and Talmud, the following prefixes are used.

| | |
|---|---|
| m. | Mishnah |
| b. | Babylonian Talmud |

# DIVORCE, DIVORCÉ, AND DIVORCÉE

In order to distinguish easily and quickly between "**divorce**" (verb/noun) and "**divorcé**" (person/masculine) and "**divorcée**" (person/feminine), throughout this book "**divorcée**" (person/feminine), will be used instead of "**divorcé**" (person/masculine) except where the masculine usage is warranted.

# TABLE OF CONTENTS

# PREFACE

Chantal, the wife of my youth (my first and only wife) and I are happily married. We have four wonderful children, have weathered many storms together by God's grace, and enjoy being with each other today as much as when we were first married in August of 1988, even more-so if that is possible. Like any married couple, we have had our share of problems, and we are not too proud to seek help when needed. Thankfully, God has enabled us to remain faithful to each other. Though neither of us has ever been divorced, both sets of our parents, three of our siblings, and numerous extended family members have experienced divorce. Thus, we are well acquainted with the pain of divorce; but we have also witnessed the power of God's grace in healing broken lives and relationships.

I have been asked repeatedly concerning my motivation for writing on this controversial subject and for presenting such a nontraditional doctrine of marriage, divorce, and remarriage. In one word, I answer—Freedom! In 1984, I had a life-changing experience; I was born-again and filled with the Holy Spirit. Prior to this event in my life, I was a "religious" person, but I did not have a personal relationship with God. I was raised in a church that taught that the Baptism in the Holy Spirit as experienced by many in the New Testament was for the first century church, but not for today. Relationship with God was based upon obedience, rather than obedience being based upon relationship. Salvation was dependent upon the way that I lived my life, as opposed to the way that I lived my life being based upon my salvation.

Meeting and getting to know people who had experienced the Baptism in the Holy Spirit radically challenged my beliefs. After several months of researching the Bible concerning the Baptism in the Holy Spirit, I was born again and filled with the Holy Spirit. This event changed my understanding of God, salvation, and life. No longer did I obey in order to be saved; I obeyed *because* I was saved. I then assumed that if I had been taught errant doctrine concerning such foundational concepts as salvation and the Baptism in the Holy Spirit, then other doctrines that I had been taught since childhood might also be erroneous. I decided to review many of these doctrines, submit them to the Lord, and see what He had to say about them in the Word and by His Spirit.

One topic I soon restudied was marriage, divorce, and remarriage. I came to believe that there are significant errors in the traditional doctrine of marriage and divorce. Marriage is not indissoluble. God recognizes marriages that do not fit the divine ideal of a monogamous faithful lifelong union of a man and woman; and it is not sinful for divorcées to marry again *regardless* of the reasons for their previous divorces.

Frankly, I embraced these beliefs though I could not reconcile them with Jesus' difficult statements on divorce. My beliefs were also contrary to the teachings of both churches that I had been associated with, the church of my youth and the church that I joined after being Baptized in the Holy Spirit. The traditional, plain, straightforward interpretation of Jesus' words just did not make sense to me in the light of Jesus' character, His related teachings and ministry pattern, and what was taught in the remainder of the Bible. Nor did they make sense in the light of God's grace, mercy, and forgiveness (as personally experienced and understood). I did not realize at the time how a lack of knowledge concerning the historical and cultural context of Jesus' words predisposes one to misinterpret these difficult passages. Jesus clearly supported the divine ideal of marriage; but in no way do His words support several of the foundational precepts of the traditional doctrine of marriage, divorce, and remarriage. In fact, they contradict them!

Since adopting these beliefs, I have taken note of many people who were brought into some form of bondage (mental, emotional, spiritual, and/or relational) because of accepting as truth the traditional doctrine of divorce. There is a beautiful verse that refers to Jesus in the song *People Need the Lord*—"At the end of broken dreams, He's the open door." Sadly, the traditional doctrine of divorce portrays Jesus as a "closed door" for the divorcée. If divorcées accept as truth the traditional doctrine of divorce, their dreams of life-long loving marital relationships are shattered. Without remarrying their ex-spouses, for divorcées, the only hope of ever again enjoying the covenant union of marriage is dependent upon the death of their former spouses. What a terrible closed door!

Before getting into the book, I would like to affirm my belief in and love for the church, universal and local. Christ established the church for the blessing of all of mankind. Jesus loves the church, and we need to embrace His love for the church as our own. Not to love the church, the body of Christ on the earth is not to love Jesus! Of course, the church is made up of people; and anything with people in it, this side of heaven, will be far from perfect.

Every Christian should be involved actively in a local church. Jesus gave us spiritual leaders—apostles, prophets, evangelists, pastors, and teachers—so that we all can be built up in our faith and knowledge of Jesus, until as the body of Christ, we become a powerful and dynamic expression of Jesus on earth (Ephesians 4:11).

Through larger corporate gatherings of the church, we can experience a holy dimension of God Most-High—Creator of the Universe and Judge of all mankind; His grandeur and glory is marvelously revealed. In smaller gatherings of the church we can encounter the intimate and personal God Most-Nigh—our Father in heaven and the Shepherd of our souls. Jesus is truly the One and Only God of the Universe; and yet, He is our Father, Brother, and Friend. Please keep in mind as we discuss the traditional doctrine of divorce that the church is not the problem; the problem is demonic spiritual and mental strongholds that have plagued the church since the second century.

As I have shared my beliefs with Christians from various denominations, I have been amazed at the wide range of responses that I have received. Some people whole-heartedly agree and want to know why I can state with such conviction that the traditional doctrine of divorce is seriously flawed. Some are cautious and perplexed, questioning my motives. Many quickly assume, incorrectly so, that I am trying to justify a previous divorce or thinking of divorce. Others are concerned that my beliefs on this issue will in some way weaken existing marriages or empower people to "justify" their divorces. A few have been angry with me for challenging a doctrine that they have believed and taught for so long. I do not know where you may fall in this gamut of responses, but I hope that you will prayerfully consider with an open mind and heart what is written herein.

From experience, I have found that when beliefs are solidified, no amount of reason or proof will change them (sadly so). It usually takes an encounter with God to change firmly held beliefs, especially those that we have been taught since childhood. Many times a tragic event in our lives, or the lives of our loved ones, helps us recognize our need of God and this recognition motivates us to pray and study the Bible which positions us for an encounter with Him. Tragic events also work to break our hearts, making us more receptive to the Word of God.

It is when we realize our need of God that we are willing to turn from our prideful, twisted beliefs and lifestyles and turn to Him. Jesus repeatedly said, "Those that have ears to hear, let them hear." We should each seek to acquire an increasingly open mind and heart to receive from God. The fabric of an open mind is humility; and the essence of an open heart is compassion. Humility begins with admitting that we could be wrong. Compassion is birthed when we embrace the pain and suffering of others.

# INTRODUCTION

*God Is A Divorcé Too! A Message of Hope, Healing, and Forgiveness* is an academic (theological and scholarly) and pastoral (inspirational and compassionate) study of the controversial subject of marriage, divorce, and remarriage. Is divorce a sin? Is marriage a sacrament, under ecclesiastical authority, and indissoluble as commonly taught in a majority of denominations and independent churches? The divine ideal of marriage is a monogamous, exclusive, life-long union of a man and woman in a healthy interdependent familial relationship. But does God recognize marriages that do not fit that ideal? Are there morally acceptable reasons for divorce? May a divorcée marry again with God's blessing? What should the church's position be concerning divorce and remarriage? These are just a few of the questions answered in this book.

For divorcées, this book promotes freedom–religious, mental, emotional, spiritual, and relational. For children of divorce, this book brings healing and restoration. For singles, this book equips you with a spiritual and practical understanding of marriage that will help you establish a happy home, if you marry. For pastors who have a passion to bring healing to divorcées, this book equips you to minister the grace, healing, forgiveness, and hope found in the Gospel of Jesus Christ. For theologians, this book may serve as a springboard to a more in-depth study of the doctrine of marriage, divorce, and remarriage. For married couples, this book will inspire you to seek God, encourages you to walk in love and yet establish strong personal boundaries. These are accomplished through the presentation of a renewed biblical doctrine of marriage, divorce, and remarriage that is liberating and yet convicting. This renewed biblical doctrine is based firmly in the historical, cultural, social, authorial, and literary context of related biblical passages. On top of that, it just makes sense!

# Chapter 1

# GOOD NEWS FOR THE DIVORCÉE

Good news for all divorcées! God loves you and His grace and forgiveness is for you. If you are now single again, He understands your need for companionship and will provide for it. God does not expect you to live single the remainder of your life, unless He has given you the gift of celibacy. He does not expect you to try and get back with your former spouse, unless you both desire such and neither of you has subsequently remarried. If you have married again, He will bless your marriage and help you and your spouse make a go of it, if you but follow His loving care and guidance. God will even help you deal with all of the troubling baggage from your previous relationships.

God understands the pain of divorce, having experienced it Himself! Through the prophet Jeremiah, God said *"I knew that the kingdom of Israel had been unfaithful and committed many sins, yet I still hoped she might come back to me. But she didn't, so I divorced her and sent her away"* (Jeremiah 3:8 CEV). (emphasis mine) Yes, God is a divorcé too, although through no fault of His own!

God even forgives you if you were the sole cause of your marriage breaking up. He loves you intensely and desires to bless you and your relationships, bringing forgiveness, healing, restoration, and hope back into your life. He will take what the devil has meant for evil and turn it for good. If you will only trust and obey Him, He will lead you into a future filled with overflowing love, joy, and peace—His Kingdom. Some people, even some Christians and churches, might reject you; but He accepts you!

Some people will find the above statements disturbing, to say the least. Some will find them perplexing, asking "Why would he say such things, aren't they obvious?" Others fully agree with what I have said, believing in the grace and forgiveness of God, but they cannot reconcile apparent contradictory statements by Jesus. Responses vary so dramatically because what was just stated directly contradicts the "traditional Christian doctrine of marriage, divorce and remarriage" (henceforth called the "traditional doctrine of divorce").

The traditional doctrine of divorce leads one to say the following:

*God loves you and forgives you, but if you are now divorced and single again, you must live celibate the remainder of your life, unless you had a "scriptural" divorce. A "scriptural" divorce is most commonly understood as a divorce caused by adultery and possibly by abuse or abandonment, and the errant spouse's continued long-term refusal to repent.*

*If you had a "scriptural" divorce, you might be able to marry again, if you can find a minister willing to perform the wedding ceremony. If you had an "unscriptural" divorce and you have remarried, I'm sorry, but God does not recognize your marriage and you are living in adultery. In fact, you are still married to your former spouse "in the eyes of God." In order to get right with God, you need to divorce your current spouse and either live celibate the remainder of your life, or remarry your former spouse if possible. If you caused your first divorce because of adultery, you're "up the creek without a paddle" and relegated to a life of celibacy as punishment for your sins. If your spouse divorces you for unscriptural reasons, you too must live celibate the remainder of your life because of his/her sin. If you have children and fit one of the cases where you must remain celibate, I'm sorry, but your children are relegated to living in a single parent home because of your sin and/or the sin of your spouse.*

Thankfully, though most Christian denominations espouse the traditional doctrine of divorce, many ministers do not *enforce* it on the people in their care. Rather, many tend to ignore this doctrine and focus on the grace and forgiveness of Christ. Some find a way to work around it, interpreting Jesus' words as overstatements meant to counter the hypocritical teachings of the Pharisees. Still others sidestep the issue by not directly addressing the doctrine, much less teaching it, evasively pointing people to scripture and instructing them to make up their own minds.

Due to the traditional doctrine of divorce, many Christians who have had a civil divorce are not "allowed" to remarry with the "blessing" of the church unless their first marriage is annulled. To annul a marriage is to declare it invalid. An annulment "is a decree that marriage attempted by a couple was illegal or invalid according to the rules of the society and therefor was not in fact a marriage."[1] A married couple who divorced and then had the marriage annulled, is then considered by the church to have never been married, even if the couple had children together. As the number and percentage of divorces in America has dramatically increased over the last thirty years, so has the number of annulments. To some, this might seem like a strange way of dealing with the problem of marriages breaking up. But if you accept as a doctrinal truth that marriage is indissoluble, then annulment is the only option that will free previously married people to remarry with the blessing and acknowledgement of the church.

Problems and questions abound surrounding the traditional doctrine of divorce; and there is often a significant disconnect between the traditional doctrine and its practical application in the lives of people. Why? Because the traditional doctrine of divorce is based on error, being made up of multiple interconnected erroneous beliefs and subtle, but tragic, misinterpretations of scripture. This has created a spider's web of deception that has many people captured in false religious bondage, keeping them from experiencing the freedom that is in Christ and the relational redeeming power of the Gospel! In order to dissolve this web of deceit, freeing those wrapped in it, we will need to examine closely each strand and expose the error and deception at its core.

It is traditionally believed that in God's sight, a person's first marriage is his/her only legitimate marriage; and except for death or a "scriptural" divorce (one based on adultery or the Pauline Privilege[2]), God does not recognize subsequent marriages. Therefore, people who divorced their previous spouses for "unscriptural" reasons and married another are in illegitimate, immoral relationships, and are actually living in adultery. In order to come into or remain in fellowship with God and the church, divorcées with "unscriptural" divorces that have not remarried should either seek to remarry their first spouse or live celibate the remainder of their lives or until their former spouses die. Some ministers and theologians who believe the traditional doctrine of divorce go so far as to say that people whose divorces were "unscriptural" who have remarried are now in marriages not recognized by God and must now divorce their current spouses even if they now have children through these relationships. The people then must either remarry their first spouses or remain celibate the remainder of their lives.

This false doctrine has the potential to weaken and even cripple existing marriages especially among those who have been divorced and remarried. Christian divorcées who have remarried are led to question the viability of their marriages asking, "Is my marriage recognized by God or am I living in sin? Is my marriage an adulterous relationship?" Not only that, but the doctrine of the indissolubility of marriage actually weakens marriages instead of strengthening them. Which is treated with more care and honor, a cast-iron (indissoluble) pot or a fragile (breakable) China vase?

The traditional doctrine of divorce has helped to increase the already overwhelming levels of fear and emotional turmoil in Christians who are caught in destructive or abusive marriages. Furthermore, it has significantly handicapped the church in reaching the lost with the Gospel, especially single divorcées and those who have remarried. For divorcées who have embraced this doctrine and remained celibate, it has cut them off from the blessings of marriage. Few people are born with, or grow to have, no desire or need for the loving committed companionship of married life. Divorce is devastating enough without the church pouring salt in the wounds of those who have felt its jagged cutting edge.

Jesus said that if we abide in Him and His Word, we will know the truth and the truth will set us free (John 8:31). Truth brings freedom from sin. Doctrinal error, false teachings, and false religions increase our slavery to sin. Understanding and accepting the truth regarding marriage, divorce, and remarriage can only help to free us from sin, individually and corporately.

The title of this book, *God is a Divorcé Too!* is based upon Jeremiah 3:8 where the prophet Jeremiah quotes God saying that He divorced Israel. In no way is this book meant to malign God or be sacrilegious! Its purpose is to challenge radically the traditional doctrine and the negative beliefs, attitudes, and feelings that many Christians have towards divorcées! Divorce is often subconsciously equated with sin and failure, regardless of its justification. Therefore when one says, "God is a divorcé too," it's as if one is speaking evil of God.

Sadly, in many Christian fellowships, to be labeled a divorcée is to be considered someone on the fringe of acceptability, at best. At worst, it means to be rejected and completely excluded. A friend of mine in the U.S. Navy shared with me the following.

When I move to a new area and start attending a new church, the "Absolute Last Thing" (his verbal emphasis) that I hope ever comes out about my wife and I is that we have both been divorced and are now in our second marriage. People treat us differently; some avoid us like the plague.

My friend, his wife, and their children are devoted Christians and tremendous assets to any fellowship of believers. It is shameful and tragic that any Christian, much less complete congregations should treat them in such a manner. This evil is the fruit of the traditional doctrine of divorce.

The church should be the one organization above all others through whom divorcées are made to feel accepted and loved. Far too often, the church causes divorcées to feel excluded, shamed, and wrongly judged. Just ask a few Christian divorcées! Divorce is not a blight on the church; but arrogant and self-righteous attitudes are! Many people that are not raised in the church come to Christ due to recognizing their need of God through tragic losses in their lives. The first step towards salvation is admitting our need of God. For many people, divorce is the loss that drives them to their knees in search of God. The church needs to be there in their time of need, offering the forgiveness, hope, and restoration that is found only in Christ. For the Christian, should the church provide any less? I think not!

Jesus numbered Himself with sinners, and often those of the vilest sort felt comfortable in His presence. The few people that He openly rebuked were the self-righteous, hypocritical religious leaders of His day! Sadly, the opposite is true in some churches, where "sinners" are made to feel like dirt.

Why the title, *God is a Divorcé Too*!? First of all, it is a valid scriptural metaphor of God, although obscure, being used only once in the Bible. Jeremiah prophetically quotes God saying;

*The kingdom of Israel was like an unfaithful wife who became a prostitute on the hilltops and in the shade of large trees. I knew that the kingdom of Israel had been unfaithful and committed many sins, yet I still hoped she might come back to me. But she didn't, so I divorced her and sent her away* (Jeremiah 3:6-9 CEV). (emphasis mine)

Of course, God's relationship with Israel is much more involved, theologically speaking, than just thinking of God as a divorcé. In Jeremiah's day, Israel was a divided kingdom with Israel's ten tribes to the North and Judah's two tribes in the South. Thus, when God spoke of having divorced Israel, He was still married to a remnant of His covenant people, Judah. The purpose of the analogy was to call Judah (the remnant of Israel) back to faithfulness in her relationship with God, affirming God's love for His people. This passage is not meant to say that God has or ever will give up on Israel as a people.

The Apostle Paul gives an extensive discourse on God's continuing love for and relationship with Israel in Romans chapters nine, ten, and eleven. Has God put away Israel as a whole? Absolutely not! God has reserved for Himself a remnant, a group of faithful Jewish believers that have or will accept Jesus, the Messiah! The Apostle Paul wrote,

> *I say then, has God cast away His people? Certainly not! For I also am an Israelite, of the seed of Abraham, of the tribe of Benjamin. God has not cast away His people whom He foreknew. Or do you not know what the Scripture says of Elijah, how he pleads with God against Israel, saying, "LORD, they have killed Your prophets and torn down Your altars, and I alone am left, and they seek my life"? But what does the divine response say to him? "I have reserved for Myself seven thousand men who have not bowed the knee to Baal." Even so then, at this present time there is a remnant according to the election of grace* (Romans 11:1-5 NKJV). (emphasis mine)

In no way is the title of this book, *God Is A Divorcé Too!*, meant to empower anti-Semitism in the church. In fact, several aspects of this study highlight the need for non-Jewish believers to respect and value our Jewish heritage. This book is not a theological discourse on God's relationship with the nation of Israel today. It is strictly a rebuttal to the traditional doctrine of divorce, presenting what I believe to be a renewed biblical theology of marriage, divorce, and remarriage.

God being a divorcé is a valid scriptural metaphor, one that we can receive much encouragement and grace from. *"All Scripture is given by inspiration of God, and is profitable for doctrine, for reproof, for correction, for instruction in righteousness, that the man of God may be complete, thoroughly equipped for every good work"* (II Timothy 3:16 & 17 NKJV). The metaphor of God being a divorcé is thus profitable to be taught, to correct our thinking, and to instruct us in right living so that we may be completely equipped to administer the grace of God in word and deed!

The title, *God is a Divorcé Too!,* radically challenges (at a gut level) one's subconscious beliefs, attitudes, values, and feelings concerning divorce and divorcées. Obviously, one does not use a metaphor as a foundation for doctrine; but any biblical metaphor of God that is at odds with our beliefs, or that causes us to be uncomfortable, should cause us to seriously and prayerfully reconsider our beliefs.

The following is a simple geometric puzzle that illustrates this concept. Please take a few minutes to solve it before reading further and looking at the solution. Simply (1) connect all nine dots in the following diagram, (2) use only four straight lines, and (3) once you start drawing, do not lift your pencil or retrace another line segment. Go!

Most people cannot readily solve this puzzle because they subconsciously believe and adhere to limits that are not stated. When a person believes something, information or options that do not agree with that belief are typically rejected with little or no consideration. In the previous diagram, one naturally sees a box and subconsciously adheres to an unstated rule that he must remain within that box in order to solve the puzzle. *"Unstated"* is the key word here. There is no such rule. It is an assumed limitation, a subconscious belief.

In order to solve this puzzle, one must think "outside of the box." The solution is actually quite simple once you think "outside of the box." In the following diagram, the "box" has been shaded in order to identify easily the original nine dots. Start with point **A**, trace the line following the arrows to points **B, C, D**, and back to **B**. Note that there are only four line segments, but points **C** and **D** are "outside of the box."

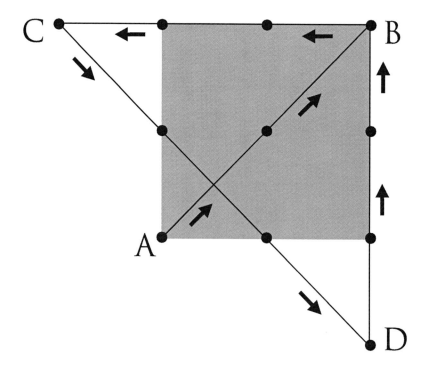

In like manner, the scriptural metaphor of "God being a divorcé" is extremely outside of the box of beliefs, values, and attitudes that most Christians have concerning divorce. Most of our assumptions and beliefs are so deeply ingrained that we quickly disregard, discredit, and even vehemently oppose any information or concept that contradicts them. When information does not fit within our box, we have a choice to make–either discredit and disregard it, or get a bigger box. Concerning the doctrine of marriage, divorce, and remarriage, I propose that we find a bigger box, one that incorporates all of the teachings in the Bible, including the metaphor of God being a divorcé.

Jesus purposefully did and said things that would challenge the religious traditions of His day that did not fit the character, Spirit, or Law of God. The title, *God Is A Divorcé Too!,* also does this, dynamically challenging the traditional doctrine of divorce, its negative attitudes and beliefs! The traditional doctrine of marriage and divorce fosters these negative attitudes, being founded on human rules and not the commands of God. The traditional doctrine is in the same category as the hypocritical teachings of the Pharisees. Speaking to the Pharisees, Jesus said,

> *Isaiah was right when he spoke about you hypocrites. He wrote, "These people show honor to me with words, but their hearts are far from me. Their worship of me is worthless. The things they teach are nothing but human rules." You have stopped following the commands of God, and you follow only human teachings* (Mark 7:6-9 NCV). (emphasis mine)

The metaphor of God being a divorcé too, can inspire, encourage, strengthen, comfort, and give hope to the divorcée. Understanding God as a divorcé has great potential to bring healing and restoration to many that struggle with an overwhelming sense of failure and hopelessness due to their own divorce or that of a loved one.

God understands the pain of divorce and will heal the broken-hearted if we will but turn to Him. Even though God is the perfect husband, his wife (Israel) rejected Him, running off with other lovers. Was this due to God being at fault in any way? Obviously not! In like manner, a man or woman can be a godly spouse, contributing little, if any, to the breakup of their marriage; and in no way should divorce, in and of itself, be a mark against his or her character. Symbolism is a powerful means of communication. God identifies with the heartbreak of divorce, having experienced it Himself!

Following this paragraph and scattered throughout this book are real-life examples of people in bondage, wrapped in a web of deceit—the traditional doctrine of divorce. In an effort to protect their identities, actual names are not used. These are added to this book in order to highlight the every-day sadistic consequences that the traditional doctrine of divorce has had and *is* having in the lives of people.

### HENRY AND SARAH

Henry, one of the leaders in a small Christian congregation, fell into an affair with Sarah, a woman in his congregation. He ended up divorcing his wife, leaving her and their children, marrying and starting a new family with Sarah. He later repented of his sins against his first wife and children, sought and received forgiveness from them, and greatly desired restoration in his relationship with God. But for over fifteen years, he lived under a vexing sense of grief, guilt, and self-condemnation. He would not go back to church because he did not want to be hypocritical. "Why would he think this?" you might ask.

Henry believed that to be fully restored in his relationship with God and the church, he needed to divorce Sarah, his second wife, and live celibate the remainder of his life. He believed that God did not recognize his second marriage and that he was actually living in adultery. This was the doctrine that his church embraced–the traditional doctrine of divorce. Thankfully, he loved his second wife and family too much to do that to them. Two wrongs just do not make a right!

Within the last few years, he has begun to work through this with the help of another church, one that does not fully embrace the traditional doctrine of divorce. With his family, he now faithfully attends that church and is overcoming the shame, grief, guilt, and self-condemnation that has plagued him for so long.

The good news to Henry and anyone else in a similar situation is that God has forgiven you, and does not expect you to break up your family. Actually, God desires for you to draw close to Him; and He will give you the strength, wisdom, love, and provision to be a blessing to both families, and, of course, remain faithful to your current wife. God not only recognizes your second marriage, but He has and will continue to bless it. God will even bring healing to the wounds you have caused in others, and bring restoration to your relationships. Only accept His forgiveness and seek after Him with all of your heart! People who receive much forgiveness, in turn, love God and others all the more!

The traditional doctrine of divorce asserts that marriage is a sacrament, under ecclesiastical authority, and indissoluble. It is commonly believed that Jesus desired to repudiate the Law of Moses on divorce, legislatively making divorce unacceptable and unrecognized by God (except possibly for adultery). The Apostle Paul's teaching on marriage is also understood by many as legislative in nature, adding an acceptable reason for divorce called the Pauline Privilege–abandonment by an unbelieving spouse. All of these assertions of the traditional doctrine of marriage and divorce are false. The error at the heart of each statement is exposed in the following chapters.

# Chapter 11
# ONE FLESH

How one *defines* marriage is foundational to the theology of marriage. *What is marriage?* It is a covenant-based relationship whereby a man and woman are legally and socially united for the purpose of establishing a new family. It is "the institution whereby men and women are joined in a special kind of social and legal dependence for the purpose of founding and maintaining a family."[3] Clearly, the "divine ideal" for marriage is that of a monogamous, mutually faithful and loving, life-long union of a man and woman in an interdependent, legally sanctioned, familial relationship (Genesis 2:24, Matthew 19:5); and what God has joined together should not be broken apart by man (Matthew 19:6).

Shortly before Chantal and I were to wed, I was consumed with anxiety, afraid that I would not be able to support us financially. At the time, I had trouble providing for my own needs, much less for those of another person. What if a child came along soon? To complicate matters, I had just been informed that I was to be laid-off from my job the day before our wedding. All I could think of was "double the responsibility, double the financial burden, Double-the-Trouble!" Fear was "eatin' my grits!"

Thank God, I had recently learned that the root of all fear is a lie; so I closed myself away in prayer asking God to reveal what lie I had accepted as truth. After some time in worship and prayer, the Holy Spirit asked me a question, "What is your one job?" Immediately, I recalled Matthew 6:33, *"Seek first the kingdom of heaven and all these things will be added to you."*

In this passage Jesus admonishes His hearers to be not anxious concerning the most basic necessities of life: food, clothing, and housing. Why, because our Father in heaven knows our needs and promises to meet them if we but seek first His Kingdom!

I then received a vision of myself carrying a white five-gallon bucket full of water. This was my "one job." The Holy Spirit then said to me, "The lie is 'Double-the-Trouble.'" Upon hearing this, I received another vision of myself. This time, Chantal was with me; and we were carrying that same bucket together, between us, on a pole resting on our shoulders. In the first vision, I was a little off-balanced and moving slowly. In the second vision, Chantal and I were almost running as we carried the bucket with ease. The load was ten times lighter and immensely more balanced.

If a picture is worth a thousand words, a mental movie clip must be worth ten thousand. I realized that God had brought Chantal into my life as a wonderful blessing. He had given her as a helpmate for me, to help me in seeking first the kingdom of God! As we worked together in that pursuit, I had faith that God would provide our needs because He said that He would. Faith comes by hearing (accepting truth in our inward man) the Word of God (Romans 10:17). The Bible says that, "*He who finds a wife finds a good thing, and obtains favor from the Lord*" (Proverbs 18:22 KJV). Marriage has the potential to bring great wealth to you personally and all those whom you love.

The primary purpose of marriage is to help fulfill mankind's most basic of all psychological, spiritual, social, and emotional needs—companionship! "*The LORD God said: 'It is not good for the man to be **alone**. I will make a suitable partner for him'*" (Genesis 2:18 NAB). (emphasis mine) Adam's need for companionship was the primary reason that God created Eve. It may be inferred from this that the most common state of mankind is to live in marital relationships. For an adult to live alone for an extended indefinite period of time takes a special grace-gift from God—celibacy, a gift that relatively few have.

A secondary purpose of marriage is to fulfill the desire to have children—procreation. "*And God blessed them, and God said unto them, Be fruitful and multiply and replenish the earth"* (Genesis 1:28 KJV). Another purpose in marriage is to provide a healthy outlet for sexual passion, *"to avoid fornication, let every man have his own wife, and let every woman have her own husband"* (I Corinthians 7:2 KJV). And it is certainly *"better to marry than to burn with sexual desire"* (I Corinthians 7:9b NCV).

Noah Webster defined marriage as "the act of uniting a man and woman for life; the legal union of a man and woman for life. Marriage is a contract both civil and religious, by which the parties engage to live together in mutual affection and fidelity, till death shall separate them. Marriage was instituted by God himself for the purpose of preventing the promiscuous intercourse of the sexes, for promoting domestic felicity, and for securing the maintenance and education of children."[4]

Marriage is an interdependent relationship whereby these and other needs and desires are fulfilled in a healthy manner. Interdependence is an interesting concept, especially as opposed to codependence. In an interdependent marital relationship, both parties maintain healthy personal boundaries and yet share their lives together. Neither party is consumed or overrun by the other. Both have strong independent identities, and yet together they create a corporate identity, a healthy family.

In a codependent relationship, personal boundaries are consistently overrun. People lose their individual identities and become lost in the identities of their spouses or their marriages. Sadly, rather than dining from the same bowl of life-cereal, they feed off of each other. One spouse's emotional, physical, or mental pain gives the other spouse pleasure, gratification, or a sense of release. Concerning establishing personal healthy boundaries, I highly recommend the books entitled *Boundaries: Gaining Control of Your Life* and *Boundaries in Marriage* by Henry Cloud and John Townsend.

*"And they shall become one flesh"* (Genesis 2:24b NKJV). Unfortunately, having strong personal boundaries in marriage is not taught in most churches. This error is under-girded to some degree by a misinterpretation of the phrase "one flesh." This phrase is commonly interpreted to mean that through marriage two people undergo some kind of a metaphysical metamorphosis and become "like one person." The Contemporary English

Version even translates the aforementioned passage, "and the two of them become like one person" as if they experience a supernatural joining or union that blends them into a single homogenous mass.

I have even heard a famous television minister say that when a couple leaves the altar of marriage, "God either sees both of them or neither of them!" What a tragic misinterpretation of scripture! In what way does the couple become "like one person," physically, legally, socially, emotionally, spiritually, or mentally? In no way do they become "like one person." In the Bible, in Hebraic and Aramaic cultures, the term *"flesh"* was used to refer to one's clan or family group. For example, a law concerning slavery in Leviticus 25:49 says, *"or their uncle or their uncle's son may redeem them, or anyone **of their family** who is **of their own flesh** may redeem them"* (NRSV). (emphasis mine)

To "become one flesh" is synonymous with becoming one family. The meaning and emphasis of Genesis 2:24b, *"and the two shall become one flesh,"* is the creation of a new and separate family unit, not the creation of a new creature or state of being. The man leaves his father and mother, his original family, and cleaves to his wife; the two then become "one flesh," creating a new family, the most basic social unit of human society. "One flesh" does not imply in any way that two individuals become like one person, losing any aspect of their individual identities. Nor does it imply that the two are inseparably joined like Siamese Twins who share the same vital organs. It is more like two horses that have been yoked together in order to work as a team. The yoke that binds them together is real, tangible, and weighty; but their personal identities are not compromised.

In the New Testament, the Apostle Paul uses the phrase "one flesh" as an analogy to condemn fornication (immoral sexual relationships). He says:

> The **body** is meant not for fornication but for the Lord, and the Lord for the **body**. And God raised the Lord and will also raise us by his power. Do you not know that your **bodies are members of Christ**? Should I therefore take the **members of Christ** and make them **members of a prostitute**? Never! Do you not know that whoever is united to a prostitute **becomes**

*one body* with her? For it is said, "The two shall be *one flesh*." But anyone united to the Lord becomes **one spirit** with him. Shun fornication! Every sin that a person commits is outside *the body*; but the fornicator sins against *the body* itself. Or do you not know that your **body** is a temple of the Holy Spirit within you, which you have from God, and that you are not your own? For you were bought with a price; therefore glorify God in your **body** (I Corinthians 6:13b-20 NRSV). (emphasis mine)

The cultural context of this passage is significant. In Corinth, more than one thousand prostitutes performed their trade in "honor" of Aphrodite, servicing the sexual lust of the "worshippers," and raising financial support for the temple to their false god. This passage is therefore a passionate plea for Christians to be sexually pure, especially in regards to these prostitutes. Fornication is sinful enough without joining **the body**, the "family" of Christ, with the "family" of Aphrodite! Fornication is a sin against your own person as well as a sin against the body of Christ. It is a sin that is uniquely evil in its scope and ramifications–physically, spiritually, and emotionally! However, "to be one flesh" does not imply that the person and the prostitute become like one person before God!

"One flesh" has often been used to underscore the need for and power of unity in marriage. It is true that the more unity a married couple attains in beliefs, values, purpose, and mutual respect and love, the healthier they are as a couple and as individuals. This is a very important principal truth; however, the phrase "one flesh" does not mean that they become like one person in any way. It simply means that they create a new family.

Like the facets of a diamond, there are many aspects to a marital relationship: emotional, psychological, physical, economic, sexual, spiritual, social, parental, and legal. These facets are distinct and yet overlap and influence each other significantly.

The **emotional** dimension of marriage involves feelings of love, hate, anger, joy, peace, depression, acceptance, and rejection. Emotions are a powerful motivation in our lives. In modern culture, emotion is usually the first place of relational unity and/or separation. Good or bad, we place a high priority on the way we feel and the way another person influences our feelings. If we feel loved, wanted, and accepted in a person's presence, we are drawn to him/her. If we feel hated, neglected, overlooked, or rejected, we are repulsed. A question married people need to ask themselves periodically is, "How do I make my spouse feel?" We must also realize that our spouses are not ultimately responsible for the way we feel. Our spouses are capable of significantly influencing our emotional state; but the way we feel is much more dependent upon our choices, what we choose to think about, and how we choose to live. If you don't bring happiness *into* marriage, you won't find it there!

The **psychological** aspect of a relationship is primarily rooted in the subconscious mind. The difference between our conscious and subconscious thought-life is similar to the difference between a computer's hard drive and its RAM. The hard drive contains all of the installed programs and data. It determines how information is managed, interpreted, evaluated, and stored— our subconscious mind. RAM is where the active processing of information occurs—our conscious mind. RAM activity is entirely based on the programming in the hard drive. In the same way, our conscious processing of information is entirely based on our subconscious beliefs, values, and attitudes.

Our subconscious programming (our foundational knowledge, beliefs, and assumptions about God, the world, other people, and ourselves) determines how we process information that we receive through our senses. Understanding others requires that we interpret their words, actions, tone of voice, and body language. What we often fail to realize is that our understanding is almost entirely based on our subconscious beliefs and assumptions!

The psychological union is important in any relationship, especially in marriage. What are the foundational beliefs that we have about our spouses, marriages, and ourselves? Do we believe that our spouses love us more than anyone or anything else in the world; or do we believe that they are so wrapped up in themselves that they really don't care about us at all? Do we believe that we are or are not worthy of love? Such beliefs significantly effect how we interpret our spouses' words and actions.

**Material** bonding, the sharing of physical resources is another aspect of marriage. Most married couples live together and share the same bed. This promotes continued and increasing unity in the other facets of the marriage. Unfortunately, there is occasionally a need for a married couple to live separately, due to job requirements or other situations. Physical separation can cause tremendous stress on the marital bond.

The **economic** union of a couple is another important aspect of marriage. There are many financial considerations in selecting a spouse. How far is he/she in debt? Who will handle the finances? Can there be agreement on budgeting of resources? What does each believe about tithing and charitable donations? What financial responsibilities does he/she have due to previous relationships—child support and alimony? These are just a few of the financial concerns that should be considered *before* getting married.

An interesting ongoing debate is the use of prenuptial agreements. Some people argue that an engaged couple should not consider using a prenuptial agreement because it makes provision for divorce. Others who recognize that divorce is a possibility wish to make prior arrangements in order to keep from losing too much of the wealth that they bring into the marriage if divorce occurs. A prenuptial agreement can help establish and maintain clear economic boundaries where needed. This is especially important for those considering blending families previously split by divorce. In biblical times, the dowry shared many similar purposes of the modern prenuptial agreement. If a divorce took place, the guilty party forfeited or lost the dowry, which was a significant amount of money as determined by the socioeconomic level of the couple's family.

A fulfilling **sexual** relationship with one's spouse is also important. A healthy outlet for our sexual passion is one of the foundational purposes of marriage. The Bible teaches us to keep the marriage bed pure. Of course, purity refers to more than just acceptable and non-acceptable acts; it refers to a purity of heart and mind, as well as body. We need to approach sexual intimacy seeking to fulfill the needs of our spouses, not just our own. Another concern today is sexually transmitted diseases. With such diseases swiftly becoming epidemic, sexual purity is increasingly important in spouse selection.

As always, biblical commands are proving to be *for* our good—not to keep us *from* good!

The **spiritual** dimension of marriage provides the foundation for the relationship. Our spirits are the ultimate source of what we think, feel, say, and do. If our spirits are bitter and unforgiving, prideful and haughty, or deceitful and twisted, all manner of evil will come out of our mouths and through our actions. On the other hand, if our spirits are bathed in the life of God, then love, mercy, and grace will flow from us like a river. In this day of rampant perversion, having our hearts cleansed by the Word and Spirit of God is exceedingly important. Reading the Bible, water baptism, communion, confession, prayer, and fasting are powerful means of grace for cleansing of sin and the breaking of demonic spiritual bondage.

Jack Hayford shares the following story about the significance of Water Baptism in his book, *Newborn, Your New Life In Christ.*

I was once beside a couple who had come, along with several others, into the baptistery for baptism. I had never met the couple, but knew from the baptismal cards, they handed me that they were married. As I looked into their faces, the Holy Spirit whispered to my heart: "They have deep marital problems because of immoral acts prior to their marriage. Speak to them. I'll free them tonight as they are baptized."

To avoid embarrassing them in front of the others who also were being baptized, I drew them aside as the congregation sang a song of worship. "Please don't feel embarrassed," I told them quietly. "What I have to share is not in condemnation, but because Jesus wants these baptismal waters to be waters of deliverance for you both.

"I must be direct: The Holy Spirit has just shown me two things about you. First, you had sexual intercourse together before you were married, didn't you?" They looked at each other a moment, and then back at me. They recognized I was not judging them, but that I was seeking to help them. 'Yes,' they said together.

"Secondly, you are having real stress in your marriage—and are especially hindered in your sexual relationship." 'Right,' they said, nodding.

"Listen," I continued, "the Holy Spirit has not revealed this to shame you, but to show He is ready to free you from the bonds of past sin; a bondage you couldn't break because you didn't even know it was related to sins committed before you knew Jesus. So, right now, confess to him that you specifically reject your past way of thought that excused such action. If you can do that, you will experience a real deliverance as you are baptized tonight." We prayed briefly and then rejoined the others and proceeded with baptism. Several days later I received a beautiful letter from this couple:

*Dear Pastor Jack,*

*There are hardly words to describe the change we have realized in our lives and in our marriage. Invisible chains have been broken and freeing life and joy have entered our home and our relationship. Thank you for your sensitivity to the Holy Spirit.*

*We have been born again for six months, but were somehow hesitant to be baptized. The forgiveness we found with our salvation was no less real, but we did wonder why we were so unable to "get it all together."*

*Now Jesus has done it! Obedience to baptism coupled with the Holy Spirit's presence and power has untangled the past and opened the door to a new kind of life and marriage for us. Praise his name![5]*

As a young man, I too experienced deliverance when I was baptized in water. In my early-teens, I was introduced to pornography. During college, this became an addiction and significantly warped my mind in regards to women. My subconscious became so polluted that I could not look at an attractive woman without evil thoughts flooding my consciousness. After being born again and filled with the Holy Spirit when I was twenty-four, I began to struggle against these twisted thoughts by praying to God for deliverance, averting my eyes, and consciously wrestling to control my thoughts when I saw a beautiful woman. But it seemed like the more that I fought this tendency, the greater the struggle, and the deeper the bondage became or was revealed to be.

As I was driving to work one day, I was once again praying about this and other issues of sin in my life when the Holy Spirit said to me, "Well, be baptized." The tone of His voice was kind and gentle, yet it also had in it, a hint of "didn't you know that." I had been raised in a church that strongly emphasized water baptism, and was baptized when I was a child of nine years old. I never considered being baptized again as an adult, even though I was not truly "born again" or "born of the Spirit" until I was twenty-four. After being born of and filled with the Holy Spirit, I should have thought to have been baptized, but I did not.

The church that I attended at the time did not emphasize water baptism, only performing baptisms once a month, so several weeks later I was scheduled to be baptized. During the intervening time I forgot about the impetus for the baptism and thought primarily about inviting friends and family to the event. The big night came and went without many fanfares or any supernatural manifestations in my life. A few days later, though, I had an experience that revealed that I had indeed experienced the delivering power of God inherent in baptism for the believer.

As I walked across the parking lot at work, a beautiful young lady walking in the opposite direction passed near me. I looked at her and thought, "She's beautiful, Lord." It was like smelling a fragrant rose or appreciating a sunset. Not one lustful thought came to mind; and yet I recognized and appreciated her beauty.

I did not think much of the incident until I reached the other side of the parking lot. The Holy Spirit surprised me when He asked, "Did you see that?" I responded with an astute thought, "What?" The Holy Spirit replied, "You didn't lust after her!" In His voice, I could hear that He was excited and pleased, and He knew that I would be, too. I was overwhelmed with excitement! I could now look at a pretty woman without an overwhelming struggle of unclean thoughts. Just recalling this, I have tears in my eyes, tears of thanksgiving and relief. Jesus came to set the captives free, of whom I was one.

Do not underestimate the spiritual dimension of marriage. Spiritual bondage in one or both parties has the potential to wreak havoc in all of the other dimensions of the marriage. Yet spiritual bondage may seem totally unrelated to the problem at hand and is often hidden from self-examination or professional counseling, secular or Christian. We need Jesus and the conviction of the Holy

Spirit to uncover and deliver us from all manner of evil, especially the wicked and perverted thought patterns of our subconscious minds–iniquity.

Another practical aspect of the spiritual dimension of marriage is having a shared faith. Throughout the Bible, God's people are instructed not to marry people of other faiths. You've probably heard the saying, "A family that prays together, stays together!" Spiritual disunity can be the source of much strife and anguish in any family. If you are in a spiritually mixed marriage, honor one another, uphold your vows, pray for your spouse like there is no tomorrow, and treat him/her as you would treat Jesus. If you are considering marriage with someone of a different faith, count the cost, for it is high. "Evangelistic" dating and marriage (entering a relationship with a non-believer in order to encourage them to accept Christ) are ill advised and usually lead to disaster.

The **social** aspect of marriage is more encompassing than we realize. When a man marries, he not only marries his wife, but he also marries into her network of family, friends, and associates. This is a reality of marriage to consider seriously before saying, "I do!" Do you accept his/her family? Do they accept you? What are their core values, and can you live with them? How does your intended treat his/her parents and siblings? What are the strengths and weaknesses of the family into which you are marrying? How is your intended with his/her friends? Will the friends support or stress your marriage? These are just a few of the social concerns one needs to weigh before saying, "I do!"

If you are married, do your relatives and friends support or stress your marriage? What can you do to minimize negative input and maximize the positive? Are there people who you need to avoid? Are there any relational changes that could strengthen your marital bond? The social dynamic has great potential for influencing positively or negatively your relationship; so, be proactive concerning your marriage!

For those that are blessed with children, one of the strongest aspects of marriage is the **parental bond**. Love for your children often demands tremendous personal sacrifice of time, money, "sweat and blood." The best for the children is and should be a primary concern for any parent. Love for your children has the potential strength to keep a marriage together even when most of the other aspects of the marriage are broken with seemingly no hope of restoration. Even after divorce, when every other aspect of the relationship is dissolved, the parental bond demands some level of interaction between the ex-couple.

Marrying someone who already has children opens a whole new can of worms! What kind of a relationship do you have or want with his/her children? How old are the children? What kind of a relationship does your intended have with them? What kind of a parent is he/she? What potential struggles or problems do you foresee? Remember, only a fool will get between a momma-bear and her cubs! That applies to the daddy-bear, and especially a step-daddy-bear. It can be even more dangerous to come between a daddy and his little girl. It requires a tremendous amount of grace, healing and wisdom from the Lord to unite pieces of different broken families. You start off with pieces missing and extra pieces that just do not naturally fit together, and require a lot of shaping. This may require the professional help of a Christian counselor or pastor to work through related issues.

If the other dimensions of marriage are the slats of a wooden barrel, the **Marriage Covenant** is the set of steel rings that holds them together. It is the fundamental element that defines a relationship as a marriage. A person can have all of the wooden slats, the top, and the bottom, but without the steel rings that hold them together, there is no barrel. Sexual intercourse does not constitute a marriage. Having children together does not; nor does living together. To marry someone is "to join as husband and wife according to law or custom."[6] In the United States, where we have a plurality of customs but a common law, civil law is central in defining marriage. In other countries, social and/or familial recognition through a culturally significant ceremony may establish the marriage covenant.

Unfortunately, there is significant errant teaching in the church concerning marriage covenants. Many assume that the word "covenant" is a specific biblical term, clearly defining a relationship. However, the word "covenant," in the Bible and throughout the ancient Near East, was a broad term used to describe a wide variety of relationships: simple contracts, treaties between nations, marriages, indentured slave/master relationships, God's relationship with the nation of Israel, and God's promise not to flood the world. Furthermore, many theologians and pastors fail to recognize the contractual element of a marriage covenant.

David Instone-Brewer devotes the entire first chapter of his book, *Divorce and Remarriage in the Bible,* to discuss the contractual nature of marriage as understood in the Near East in biblical times. I highly recommend this book for further study on this and related issues. For the conclusion of chapter one, Dr. Instone-Brewer writes:

> … marriage in the Pentateuch is a contract between two families and between two individuals. This contract was often recorded in a document which included the financial arrangements, the stipulations which could lead to divorce if broken, and the financial arrangements in the event of divorce. Many of these documents have been found dating from the seventh century BCE. The details recorded in these documents, and the language which is used to record them, finds exact parallels in the Pentateuch. **The Old Testament speaks of marriage as a 'covenant' (tyrb), which was the ancient Near Eastern term for any kind of binding agreement or contract.** The correct term for a marriage agreement in the Old Testament is therefor a '**marriage contract**'. Like any other contract, this contained an agreement and penalties for breaking the agreement. The penalty for breaking the marriage contract was divorce with loss of the dowry. [7] (emphasis mine)

David Instone-Brewer makes a convincing argument supporting the assertion that, "The correct term for a marriage agreement in the Old Testament is a 'marriage contract.'" However, does the English word "contract" adequately define a marriage relationship? In English, "contract" is most commonly used as a legal term with its strength in its specificity, clarity, and declared penalties for the breaking of the contract. An ironclad contract is one in which there are no loopholes or means of breaking the contract without penalty. The word "contract" usually applies to tangible and measurable elements of a relationship such as finances, responsibilities, and/or material ownership. The word "contract" also has the connotation of an insensitive, cold, calculating, and business-type relationship. However, marriage is far more than the English word "contract" can define or connote.

The English word "covenant" is a better term for describing the marriage union, though having virtually the same meaning as the word "contract." Covenant is more of a relational word that often implies a personal commitment of the involved parties to each other that far exceeds the financial, material, or legal aspects of the relationship. The word "covenant" is often biblically used as a broad, inclusive, and non-specific relational vow establishing new "family" ties. Furthermore, although the financial and material aspects of the covenant might be covered by a written contract and enforceable through civil law, the strength of a covenant is almost wholly dependent upon the moral character of the covenantors, the ones making the covenant.

The word "contract" is an integral part of the word "covenant;" but "covenant" is not necessarily implied in the word "contract." Contracts are specific and legally enforceable covenants, whereas the relational elements of covenants are neither specific nor legally enforceable. For example, mutual love, honor, submission, trust, and faithfulness are all elements of a Christian marriage covenant; but these are intangible, immeasurable attributes that are not legally enforceable due to their ethereal nature. Note the following diagram of the distinct implications and connotations of the English words "contract," "covenant," "vow," and "word."

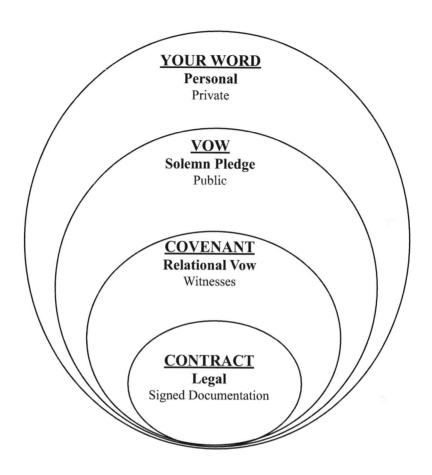

By the time of Jesus, the Jews had developed an elaborate system of vows. This was based upon the Third Commandment to not take The Name of the Lord in vain (Exodus 20:7) and other commandments to be careful not to swear falsely in The Name of the Lord (Leviticus 19:12, and Deutcronomy 23:21). The problem was that this system of oath taking actually formed a basis for lying and deception, making many "vows" not binding. Jesus condemned this system of vows and spoke concerning the need for integrity to be a vital part of one's character.

*Again, you have heard that the Law of Moses says, "Do not break your vows; you must carry out the vows you have made to the Lord." But I say, don't make any vows! If you say, "By heaven!" it is a sacred vow because heaven is God's throne. And if you say, "By the earth!" it is a sacred vow because the earth is his footstool. And don't swear, "By Jerusalem!" for Jerusalem is the city of the great King. Don't even swear, "By my head!" for you can't turn one hair white or black. Just say a simple, "Yes, I will," or "No, I won't." Your word is enough. To strengthen your promise with a vow shows that something is wrong* (Matthew 5:32-37 NLT).

If you are a person of integrity, a "man of your word," vows, covenants, and even contracts are not necessary to either force you to keep your word, or enable others to believe what you say. Your word is your bond. You will keep your word because of who you are, even if it is to your harm. If you are not a person of integrity, no vow, covenant, or contract can completely insure that you will fulfill your promise! For a selfish man, his promise will only be fulfilled if it is to his benefit as weighed against the perceived penalties for breaking his word (whether vow, covenant, or contract). The strength of a covenant is thus equal to the excellence of the moral character of the covenantors. The stronger the moral character of the covenantors, the stronger the covenant. The weaker the moral character of the covenantors, the weaker the covenant.

Although the word "covenant" does best describe the marriage union, I hesitate to use it, especially among Christians, because errant teaching concerning the word "covenant" has helped to promote errant concepts concerning marriage and divorce. In fact, the word "covenant" has been so "spiritualized" that it has lost much of its practical meaning and application. What do I mean by spiritualized? Various covenants that God established with mankind are incorrectly used as a standard for defining and describing fundamental elements of marriage covenants.

Divine covenants are often, but not always, unilateral (completely one-sided), universal, unbreakable, unconditional, and eternal. However, marriage covenants are bilateral, requiring both parties' endorsement and support. They are breakable, being conditional upon the moral character and actions of the covenantors; and temporal, ending at the dissolving of the covenant (divorce), or the death of one of the covenantors (the husband or wife).

A premier example of a divine covenant is the one Noah received. After the flood destroyed the world, and living in the ark for 375 days, Noah and his family stepped foot once again upon dry ground. God had spared them from the most devastating cataclysmic terrestrial event of all time. Overwhelmed with gratitude for God's miraculous protection, provision, and for finally standing on solid earth again, Noah sacrificed some of the clean (as in edible) animals that he had personally cared for throughout their time on the ark! This was an amazing feat when one considers that these animals were the foundation for his family's future provision. This sacrifice exhibited his radical trust in God, which pleased God greatly! The Bible then says that,

> *Then God spoke to Noah and to his sons with him, saying:*
> *"And as for Me, behold, I establish My **covenant** with you and*
> *with your descendants after you, ... Never again shall all flesh*
> *be cut off by the waters of the flood; never again shall there be*
> *a flood to destroy the earth." And God said: "This is the sign*
> *of the covenant which I make between Me and you, and every*
> *living creature that is with you, for perpetual generations: "I*
> *set My rainbow in the cloud, and it shall be for the sign of the*
> *covenant between Me and the earth* (Genesis 9:8-14 NCV).

This divine covenant is unilateral in that God makes this covenant with or without man's acceptance or agreement. It is universal in that it applies to all of mankind. It is also unbreakable, because God's moral character is without flaw. *"God is not a man that He should lie"* (Numbers 23:19 NKJV). Note that even this covenant is dependent upon the covenantor's character.

We run into problems when we try to apply the fundamental elements of this divine covenant to marriage covenants. Unlike this divine covenant, marriage covenants are in no way *uni*lateral; they are *bi*lateral, requiring the endorsement and support of *both* the husband and wife. Though the wife does everything in her power to make the marriage work, if her husband hardens his heart and legally dissolves the covenant, the marriage is broken.

Marriage covenants are also not universal, but are provincial in that their foundational assumptions and expectations are dependent upon their cultural settings or the specified elements of the covenant. For example, the marriage covenants and relationships between a polygamous husband and his wives in Saudi Arabia are different than the marriage covenant and relationship between a monogamous husband and wife in the United States of America. Different cultures have different marriage and family arrangements and covenants. Some are closer to the divine ideal than others, but that does not make the covenants any less real or binding.

Furthermore, marriage covenants are by no means indissoluble, especially when one considers the inherent depravity of mankind. It is because of this depravity, the hard-heartedness of mankind, that God inspired the bill of divorce. It facilitated the legal and social dissolution of marriages that have gone awry, and specifically enabled divorcées to remarry without fear of negative social, religious, or civil repercussions.

Marriage covenants are NOT unconditional! Though modern western marriage vows do not specify conditions upon which the marriage will be dissolved; mutual love, honor, respect, and fidelity are stated and implied in the ceremony and understood by the couple, the witnesses, the one performing the ceremony, and God. *A habitual breach of any of these elements of the covenant is a legally and morally acceptable reason for the dissolution of the marriage relationship—divorce!* Ultimately, marriage covenants are only as strong as the moral character of the covenantors. Outside factors such as family, the church, civil law, social norms, and friends have minimal influence upon the strength of marriage covenants. It is character that matters.

A modern attempt at strengthening marriages through civil legislation is the "Covenant Marriage" movement, which draws a conceptual and legal distinction between an ordinary marriage and a "Covenant Marriage." The concept of "Covenant Marriage" began as a way of teaching people to renew and strengthen their marriage commitments. A wonderful goal! Unfortunately, it is often assumed and stated that the world (as in non-Christians) views marriage as simply a legal contract, one based on rights and responsibilities and motivated by self-interest; whereas, Covenant Marriages are said to be based on unconditional love. This is an invalid distinction. These are differences in attitude that are founded upon the character of the couple, not the title on the marriage certificate.

The Covenant Marriage movement can best be understood by the legislation that it has fostered. Covenant Marriage laws generally provide that a couple can choose, at the time of marriage or later, to define their marriage as a "Covenant Marriage" as opposed to a traditional marriage. A few states, like Louisiana, currently have legislation that categorizes marriages into these two groups. Similar legislation is currently in the process of being made law in several other states.

Covenant Marriage legislation typically provides that a couple must not only obtain a marriage license, but they must also complete a specified amount of pre-marital counseling and/or courses. The couple must agree to full disclosure of all pertinent information (financial, previous relationships, biological problems, etc.) to their fiancée. They also agree to limit their divorce options through some type of increased civil oversight, possibly renouncing the use of no-fault divorce legislation. Furthermore, the couple agrees to receive extended marital counseling in the event of separation and before divorce is granted by a civil court.

Covenant Marriage legislation specifies and expands the legally enforceable aspect of the marriage relationship. Thus it expands the contractual nature of the relationship, not the covenantal aspect of the relationship. Recall that a contract's strength is in its specificity and legal enforceability, whereas a covenant's strength lies in the character of the covenantors. Therefore, shouldn't marriages established under such legislation be called "Contract Marriages" rather than "Covenant Marriages" considering that it is an attempt to strengthen marriages through specified and legally enforceable civil legislation? Of course, "Contract Marriage" sounds too legal, cold, and business-like. "Covenant Marriage" sounds much better, much more "religious."

No matter what it is called, civil legislation will not solve the problem of divorce. It might help a little, but ultimately the strength of a covenant is dependent upon the moral character of the covenantors. If a woman wants a strong marriage, she should marry a man with a strong moral character as evidenced by his lifestyle. How does he handle money? How does he respond under pressure? How strong are his relationships with God and other people—especially his family members and those in authority over him? More importantly, she must seek God for the strengthening and correcting of her personal moral character.

In modern culture there is a wide spectrum of beliefs concerning marriage and divorce. On one end of the spectrum is the traditional Christian doctrine claiming that marriage is a mystical spiritual bond of a man and woman creating an unbreakable union. The other extreme is an increasing trend of couples living together without establishing legal marriage covenants.

Should a couple be considered married without the legal recognition of that marriage by their civil government? The answer, in a word, is "No!" The Bible clearly teaches that we are to be subject to civil authorities (Romans 13:1). Does the state recognize as married a couple just living together? No! Does society at large recognize them as married? No! Would the vast majority of churches or other social institutions recognize them as married? No! Do individuals just living together consider themselves married? Not usually! The couple has not been legally joined as husband and wife. A marriage covenant has not been established; thus they are not married.

Some states still recognize common law marriages, "a marriage recognized in some jurisdictions and based on the parties' agreement to consider themselves married and sometimes also on their cohabitation."[8] These laws provide some level of legal protection for a woman in a long-term "marriage-like" relationship who has been abandoned by her "husband." Many states no longer recognize or enforce common law marriages due to the ease today of establishing a legal and binding marriage covenant.

Marriage occurs at the establishment of the marriage covenant. Without a covenant, there is no marriage. Most cultures require some type of formal ceremony and/or legal procedure in order to ratify a marriage covenant. If people choose to live together without establishing a marital covenant, they are not married in the eyes of man or God. Jesus, God in the flesh, spoke to the Samaritan woman at the well, noting that she had had five husbands, but the man she currently lived with was not her husband (John 4:18). Jesus recognized that the woman had been part of five different marriage covenants. She was also currently in a relationship that was not defined by a marriage covenant. Cohabitation and sexual intercourse do not constitute a marriage relationship; the legal establishment of a marriage covenant does.

# Chapter III
# KILLING THE KABLUCK

## DIVORCE — BREAKING THE MARITAL UNION

*She spent the first day packing her belongings into boxes, crates and suitcases. On the second day, she had the movers come and collect her things. On the third day, she sat down for the last time at their beautiful dining room table by candlelight, put on some soft background music, and feasted on a pound of shrimp, a jar of caviar, and a bottle of Chardonnay. When she had finished, she went into each and every room and deposited a few half-eaten shrimp shells dipped in caviar, into the hollow of the curtain rods. She then cleaned up the kitchen and left.*

*When the husband returned with his new girlfriend, all was bliss for the first few days. Then slowly, the house began to smell. They tried everything, cleaning, mopping, and airing the place out. Vents were checked for dead rodents, and carpets were steam-cleaned. Air fresheners were hung everywhere. Exterminators were brought in to set off gas canisters, during which they had to move out for a few days, and in the end they even paid to replace the expensive wool carpeting.*

*Nothing worked! People stopped coming over to visit. Repairmen refused to work in the house. The maid quit. Finally, they could not take the stench any longer and decided to move. A month later, even though they had cut their price in half, they could not find a buyer for their stinky house. Word got out, and eventually, even the local realtors refused to return their calls. Finally, they had to borrow a huge sum of money from the bank to purchase a new place.*

*The ex-wife called the man, and asked how things were going. He told her the saga of the rotting house. She listened politely, and said that she missed her old home terribly, and would be willing to reduce her divorce settlement in exchange for getting the house back. Knowing his ex-wife had no idea how bad the house reeked, he agreed on a price that was about 1/10th of what the house was worth, but only if she were to sign the papers that very day. She agreed, and within the hour his lawyers delivered the paperwork.*

*A week later the man and his girlfriend stood smiling as they watched the moving company pack everything to take to their new home, including the curtain rods.*[9]

A light-hearted introduction to an overwhelmingly depressing subject, though funny, this joke poignantly illustrates the fact that divorce stinks! Scripturally, there is no question that the divine ideal for marriage is a monogamous, faithful, life-long union of a man and woman in an interdependent familial relationship. Divorce in no way fits this divine ideal. Divorce is the dissolution, legal termination, and breaking of a marriage covenant. Noah Webster defined divorce as "A legal dissolution of the bonds of matrimony, or the separation of husband and wife by a judicial sentence. This is properly a divorce, and called technically, divorce *a vinulo matrimonii.*"[10]

The Hebraic word for divorce is כְּרִיתוּת , **kᵉrîythûwth**, *ker-ee-thooth,* and means "...a cutting of the matrimonial bond." This is an accurate word picture of what happens in divorce. Divorce is a legal, social, and spiritual severance of the covenant dimension of the marriage.

*Divorce is a type of death.* In physical death there is a separation of body and soul. Through divorce, there is a legal and social cutting—a separation of two people who were once united into one family unit. As previously noted there are several dimensions of the marriage union, but divorce is specifically the dissolving or dissolution of the marriage covenant. A marriage relationship may be dysfunctional in every other aspect, but as long as the covenant stands, the marriage exists.

Of course, there are serious ramifications in breaking any covenant, but the marriage covenant is uniquely important. Marriage is the foundation of family life, community life, and social order. When marriages are unstable, families and individuals become dysfunctional, and the social order is put in crisis. Marriage is so important that, in Israel through Moses, God instituted the death penalty for anyone caught in adultery, radically sinning against his/her spouse and marital covenant! (Leviticus 20:10)

The following is a simple agrarian parable of marriage and divorce and will be referenced and expanded elsewhere in the book. Please note that it is a *parable*, a fictional story illustrating a truth, a "true myth", as J. R. R. Tolkien would call it. This story is potentially offensive to some because of its revolting depiction of the consequences of divorce. I include it though, because it graphically illustrates the personal, familial, and social catastrophe of divorce.

## The Parable of the Kabluck

*One of the most interesting customs of the Mabutoo tribe of Central Africa is the Kabluck, the marriage bull. The family members of the bride and groom, all donate goods and services that are used in trade for a valuable young bull from proven stock. This bull provides a good foundation for the couple's new herd and a solid financial start for the new family. A bull with good bloodlines has the potential to foster security and wealth for the new family for generations. There seems to be a special, even supernatural, blessing upon these bulls, they usually live longer than normal, sire more calves, and seem to be more resistant to disease than other bulls with just as good bloodlines. The Kabluck also, and most importantly, serves as a living reminder of the treaty established between the two families and the marriage covenant established between the bride and groom. If for any reason, the husband or wife chooses to break their marriage covenant (divorce), the bull is killed.*

For many, divorce is often much worse than the death of a spouse in that it has the potential for far greater long-term negative effects. When someone dies, the family, friends, and churches rally to support the spouse and children who are left behind. Meals are provided. Childcare is arranged. A funeral service is organized to allow grief to be expressed and shared and the healing balm of the compassion of others is applied. Often times, financial donations are given to help cover medical and funeral expenses. If the family was fiscally prepared, insurance payments are received and they may end up financially better off than ever before.

Unfortunately, when a couple gets divorced, family, friends, and even churches struggle with knowing how to bring comfort to the divorced couple and their children. No formal ceremony is provided to allow family members to express their grief or receive the comfort of others. Meals are not provided. Children and adults are often left to sort things out on their own. And financially, the extra expenses often cause the family to undergo bankruptcy and even lose their family home.

The grief that a widow or orphan goes through is devastating; but the grief and pain that is experienced by a divorcée or children of divorce has the potential to be even greater. In death there is a natural, although painful, end to a relationship, allowing for healing and restoration to come naturally. In divorce, there is an unnatural end to the relationship between husband and wife and many times between parent and child. This unnatural end to these relationships is often the source of long-term emotional, psychological, spiritual, financial, and physical pain and suffering. To illustrate this, let us continue the aforementioned parable of the Kabluck (the marriage bull).

*In the Mabutoo tribe, if a person loses their spouse to death, the Kabluck lives on as a lasting reminder of the relationship. It is a sign of the covenant between the families and helps insure the continued interaction of the related families for the children's sake. However, if a Mabutoo couple divorces, they must kill their Kabluck, cut it into pieces, and chain everyone in both families and even close friends to pieces of the rotting flesh.*

*The size of the piece is determined by how important that relationship was to the individual at the time of the divorce. Sadly, as a rule, young children are chained to the largest pieces because much of their emotional, psychological, and spiritual development is dependent upon the health of their parents' relationship. As one would expect, these decaying pieces of flesh foster many kinds of sickness and disease that negatively affects everyone in the community, not just those who are chained.*

*Even after the flesh has rotted away, the bones and chains may be passed down for generations, unless the tribal medicine man intervenes and sets them free. Unfortunately, in some tribes, the medicine men believe that these chains actually help deter future couples from divorce. Therefore, they do little, if anything, to free the people who are currently chained. Many of the medicine men refuse to perform wedding ceremonies for, or recognize the marriages of people who have previously killed a Kabluck. They do this in an effort to punish these people for allowing the divorce and to deter others from doing the same, believing that their god has commanded them to do so. Tragically, increasing numbers of Mabutoos are ending up chained to several pieces of rotting flesh from their parents' Kablucks and their own. This has caused deadly epidemics that have wiped out entire villages.*

This parable is horrific, but accurate. Divorce usually results in devastating, long-term, and far-reaching negative emotional, financial, social, and spiritual ramifications. You've heard of people bringing "baggage" into their new relationships? Through divorce, we are talking about the potential for long-term deep-seated feelings of failure, rejection, inadequacy, grief, depression, anger, and resentment—to name just a few. Divorce usually causes the family a severe financial setback from which it can take years, even generations to recover. The psychological ramifications often take years, even decades to work through. There is an endless supply of could-haves, would-haves, and should-haves. Dashed dreams and hopes can be a source of never-ending discouragement and heart-sickness.

What do you do with the pictures? When a loved one passes away, the pictures stay on the wall as a constant source of comfort and remembrance. When a couple divorces, the walls are bare, the pictures are hidden away and even destroyed! Children are often divided between households, not knowing where to call home. What once brought great happiness now brings great sorrow. Things are never again the way they should be!

For some, the ripping apart of many loving relationships is the most devastating aspect of divorce. Divorcées are cut off from their ex-spouse's family and many of the friends they had as a couple. Social isolation can be a tremendous negative factor in the life of a divorcée and children of divorce. Spiritually, divorce can be a fiery trial of one's faith and trust in God; and may God forbid that your church holds tightly to the traditional doctrine of divorce!

If you are judged the bad-guy, you could be expelled from the congregation and blacklisted. Even if you are judged the victim, most churches are clueless in how to minister healing and restoration to you. Sadly, it is often assumed that the victim also failed in some way, and is even a potential threat to other marriages in the congregation. If the church believes the traditional doctrine, the spouse left behind, the *victim,* is relegated to a life of celibacy in order to remain in fellowship with the church. It can be difficult, if not impossible, to continue in the church fellowship when you feel like you have a big red "D" for "Divorcée" or "A" for "Adulterer" tattooed on your forehead.

If you have children and both parents desire to remain in their lives, the parental bond never ends; it only becomes more complicated and has greater potential for ongoing, never-ending strife, pain, grief, and self-condemnation. In fact, this one continuing bond often becomes the outlet for all of the toxic emotional, spiritual, and psychological "bad-blood" between the divorced husband and wife! Sadly, children are often used as pawns in a never-ending war, used as conduits of poison and hatred! This is destructive for everyone involved—especially the children and even the grandchildren.

In no way is divorce an "easy-out" in spite of any compelling or morally acceptable reasons. Divorce usually results in a long period of emotional, psychological, physical, financial, and spiritual anguish and pain for everyone touched by the relationship. So before you kill your *Kabluck, your marriage bull,* and you, your children, extended family, and close friends are chained to pieces of its dead rotting flesh; make sure there is *absolutely no way* to be reconciled!

# Chapter IV
# ROOTS ARE IMPORTANT

## History of the Traditional Doctrine of Divorce

### John and Naomi

John, a dear friend and fellow minister, shared with me his sorrow over the words and actions of one of his friends. With a voice filled with venom, his friend said to him, "You and your wife, Naomi, are going straight to hell because you have been divorced!" He then stormed off, never to speak with John again.

Eighteen, and having recently joined the Navy, John married a young lady whom he had known for only a few months. He was soon sent out to sea for eleven months. When he returned he found his wife five months pregnant, obviously by another man. Unable to cope with her adulterous and drug abusive lifestyle, one year and one month after marrying her, he divorced her. Broken hearted, he turned to alcohol.

Shortly thereafter, John was stationed in Japan and it just so happened that his new roommate was a Christian who began sharing with John his faith in Christ. John also started corresponding with his roommate's sister, a Christian named Naomi. John soon gave his heart to the Lord, was saved and filled with the Holy Spirit.

John and Naomi met two years later and after courting for about six months, they decided to get married. Naomi asked her uncle, a minister in a well-known denomination, to perform the wedding ceremony. Much to their grief, he refused because John was a divorcé. Thankfully, Naomi's pastor was willing to perform the ceremony.

Thirty-four years, three children, and two grand-children later, John and Naomi are still happily married. John is an evangelist, and Naomi is a worship leader in their local church. They have a wonderful life and ministry together and are filled with God's love for people.

After ministering in and with a church for over three years, with the pastoral leadership knowing full well of John's past divorce, one of their friends in the congregation found out John had been divorced 38 years ago. With seething anger in his voice, this "friend" broke-off their friendship declaring that John and Naomi were going to hell because they were living in adultery. The traditional theology of divorce strikes again!

The good news for John and Naomi is that God not only recognizes, but He has also blessed your marriage. Even now when I think of you, I hear *"Well done, my good and faithful servants!"* Only continue in the path that you have thus followed and you will also hear, *"Enter the mansions I have prepared for you."*

Church Fathers Tertullian and Ambrose both expressed that they preferred the extinction of the human race, to its continuance through procreation. Tertullian even claimed that marriage and adultery were not intrinsically different, but only in the degree of their illegitimacy. Saint Augustine believed that the sexual act in marriage was not sinful, but the passion that accompanies it is; thus continence in marriage was preferred. Origen had himself castrated before being ordained. Gregory the Great believed that whenever a married couple engaged in sexual intercourse for pleasure, their pleasure polluted their sexual act.

Throughout the Middle "Dark" Ages, sexual intercourse was commonly thought to be evil, in and of itself, and did not cease being so just because of marriage. Of course, this was and is a completely unbiblical concept. How could the Church Fathers come to have such a negative attitude towards marriage, the first institution ordained by God? Why would they oppose sexual intercourse to such extremes? Frankly, I am convinced that it was the result of several pagan and anti-Semitic influences within the early church.

The rejection of Christianity's Hebraic roots, subsequent errant interpretations of the writings of the New Testament, and an embracing of the predominant Greco-Roman philosophy of life, all combined to create an atmosphere of negativity towards sexual intercourse, marriage, and family. Could it be that this satanically charged atmosphere birthed false doctrines in the church? Is the traditional doctrine of marriage and divorce, one such doctrine?

It is amazing and tragic how quickly the early church rejected and renounced most of Christianity's Hebraic heritage. This happened even though the first century church was so Jewish that throughout the Roman Empire, Christianity was considered a Jewish sect. Jesus and the Apostles, including the Apostle Paul, were Jews and lived in obedience to the Mosaic Law, including the sacrifices, dietary laws, circumcision, and the feasts. Furthermore, up until the destruction of Jerusalem in AD 70, the leadership of the church was firmly in the hands of the Apostles, the leadership Council in Jerusalem, and other Jewish disciples and family members of Jesus.

Shortly after the birth of the church, however, there was a great awakening and tremendous outpouring of the Holy Spirit among the Gentiles. This was prophesied in the Old Testament and by Jesus and began being fulfilled with Peter sharing the Gospel with Cornelius, a Roman Centurion, and his family (Acts 10) and continued with Paul taking the Message throughout Asia Minor.

Even though prophesied in the Old Testament, Gentiles becoming Christians caused a great debate in the early church. Could a Gentile become a follower of Christ without being circumcised and becoming a Jew? Could Gentile converts be added to the church without also fully converting to Judaism, embracing the Mosaic Law, and the Oral Law that defined the Pharisaical Jewish way of life?

Unfortunately, Pharisees who had become believers began sowing seeds of division in the early church. They taught that Gentiles who wished to become Christians must be circumcised, fully converting to their legalistic brand of Judaism before becoming Christians. This argument culminated in a debate of the leaders of the newborn church in Jerusalem, the Jerusalem Council (Acts 15).

The Pharisees will be discussed in greater detail in the chapter entitled "Swallowing Camels." For now it is sufficient to note that they not only endorsed the written Mosaic Law, but they also held to the Oral Law, the traditions of their fathers. These traditions went beyond the Written Law, adding regulations in many areas like Sabbath and dietary practices and yet rendering other more important matters null and void. These oral traditions became a crushing burden for the people of Israel and were soundly rejected by Christ.

During this heated discussion at the Jerusalem Council, it was affirmed that salvation is by faith for both the Jew and the Gentile, and most certainly not by obedience to these crushing regulations. It was then decided that Gentile Christians, although saved by faith, should also be taught to reject idolatry and abstain from partaking in pagan fellowship rituals of eating meat sacrificed to idols. Secondly, they should be admonished to adhere to the Mosaic moral interpersonal laws, especially those concerning sex and marriage. Thirdly, Gentile Christians should be taught to respect, if not adopt, the dietary laws as taught in the Written Law which were particularized by the command not to eat blood or meat that was strangled (but not the expanded regulations of the Oral Law). Modern science is finally uncovering the reason for these laws—our health. For example, once an animal dies, septic poisoning begins immediately in the blood and shellfish are known to carry high amounts of toxins, thus the Written Law commands us to abstain from both.

This decision was based on the fact that many of the converts had a basic understanding of the Mosaic Law because it was being read each Sabbath in synagogues in every city. Like Cornelius, many of the early Gentile believers came from a sub-group of God-fearing Greeks and Romans (Acts 10) who were drawn by the monotheism of Judaism and the beauty of the teachings of Moses. Sadly, the Pharisaical believers rejected this proclamation by the Apostles and continued to sow seeds of division, demanding that Gentile believers fully convert to Judaism, particularized by circumcision.

It might seem astounding to us that these Pharisaical believers would be so prideful as to think that they knew more than the Apostles did. But we must remember that these were learned men, schooled from childhood in the Old Testament and the traditions of the fathers; whereas the Apostles were unlearned fishermen and even included a tax collector. Religious pride would have predisposed them to think more highly of themselves than they should, blinding them to the wisdom of others, and causing division to come to the Body of Christ.

Then war engulfed Palestine. Jerusalem and the Temple were destroyed in AD 70. Fifty years later, AD 120, Bar-Kochba was labeled the Messiah by Rabbi Akiva and led another revolt against Rome. Rome squelched the rebellion, and built a new city called Aelia in Jerusalem's place. On the temple site was erected another "temple" that was dedicated to Jupiter Capitolinus. A statue of Emperor Hadrian was put in place of the altar to God; and Emperor Hadrian taxed all Jews, including Jewish believers, unmercifully.

A pig's head was mounted over Bethlehem's gate and Jews were almost completely barred from that city. In response to such heavy persecution and taxation of the Jews, and the seeds of division sown by the Pharisees, the Gentile believers broke away from everything Jewish, not wanting to be identified any longer with the Jews. The Gentile church subsequently organized itself under a Gentile Bishop, Marcus. In AD 188 the Bishop of Rome institutes Easter in place of Passover. The Roman Church had fully disassociated itself from its Jewish roots in less than four generations after the birth of the church, throwing out the baby with the bath water.

For the next several hundred years, waves of anti-Semitism decimated the Jewish population in Israel. Jewish believers in Jesus were especially oppressed, being the "enemies" of Jews and the Roman government. In the fourth century AD, Emperor Constantine made Christianity the national religion. Speaking of the Jews, Constantine said, "We desire to have nothing in common with this so hated people, for the Redeemer has marked out another path for us. To this we will keep, and be free from disgraceful associations with this people."

Synagogues were burned, and massacres of Jews were frequent. The persecution of the Jews by Rome came to fruition in the Roman Church. Palestine increasingly lost its Jewish population and the church was increasingly removed from its Jewish heritage. This was a multifaceted satanic attack designed to destroy the newborn Church of the Messiah. Thankfully, the church was not destroyed; and today there is a growing movement in the church repenting of anti-Semitism in our midst and in our history, embracing our Jewish heritage, and thus reconnecting with our Jewish roots.

In the void created by rejecting the church's Jewish heritage, the non-Jew's Greco-Roman pagan heritage, philosophy, and religions significantly influenced the early Roman Church. Plato, 427–347 BC, a philosopher and educator of ancient Greece, is often considered the father of modern logic. He certainly is one of the most respected and important thinkers in Western culture. He so influenced early Christianity that it is widely accepted that "Plato dominated Christian philosophy during the early Middle Ages through the writings of such philosophers as Boethius and Saint Augustine."[11] Of course, the doctrine of Saint Augustine was the basis for much of the doctrine of the Roman Catholic Church.

Plato believed that the most basic desire of mankind is happiness and that happiness is the natural consequence of a healthy state of the soul. Moral virtue is equated to the health of the soul; so all people should want to be virtuous. Unfortunately people are often immoral resulting in sadness. Plato believed that if people realized that virtue resulted in happiness, people would naturally be drawn to virtue. Thus, for Plato, man's most basic problem is a lack of knowledge. This has been and still is a foundational assumption in much of Western thought and psychology. Sadly, lack of knowledge is not man's most basic problem, for this is easily remedied through education. Furthermore, Plato's understanding of "virtue" was far from biblical, even going so far as to endorse sodomy.

Plato also conceptually divided the soul of man into three parts: intellect, will, and passion. He promoted using the will to repress the passions and esteem the intellect. This philosophy of life is still prominent in Western culture today, even within the church. Conceptually dividing the soul of man into three parts is neither biblical, nor anti-biblical; it is simply a reasonable way of parsing the soul of man into functional groups. However, using the will to esteem the intellect and suppress the emotions is unbiblical.

Stoic philosophy also influenced the early church. It flourished from 300 BC to AD 300, beginning in Greece and quickly spreading to Rome. Stoics believed that they achieved happiness by following reason, focusing on things they could control, and freeing themselves from passions. The early Stoics were interested in logic, natural law, and to some degree, ethics. The later Stoics, such as Seneca, Marcus Aurelius, and Epictetus emphasized ethics and how it relates to freeing ourselves from passions. For the Stoics, virtue was the only good. Both of these concepts are unbiblical. Passion is a valuable part of who we are as humans. Furthermore, virtue is not the "only good;" in truth, our best is absolutely filthy, being polluted by our selfish nature. God is the only good!

Contrary to platonic philosophy, the sinful, selfish nature is man's most basic problem. This problem is only overcome through restoration in relationship with God (our most basic need) and He giving us new hearts, being born-again of His Spirit, and having our stony hearts replaced with hearts of flesh. This then begins the process of sanctification through which our souls are renewed and we receive and embrace the all-consuming passionate love of God for others and ourselves. The washing of the Word of God renews our minds so that we may have the Mind of Christ; and the Holy Spirit strengthens our volition so that we might be self-controlled and not succumb to the evil desires of our selfish nature! The Christian does not use his will to exalt his intellect and suppress his passions; rather, he seeks to be full of the Holy Spirit by faith through his relationship with Jesus Christ and be strengthened in every aspect of his soul; intellect, volition, and emotion! Passion and emotion are a powerful force and when controlled by the Holy Spirit, they can bring about much good and be a great asset to the believer.

Manichaeism was another significant influence in the early church. Although a false religion, it so influenced the early church that it is often referred to as a Christian heresy. It was founded by Manichaeus (AD 216–276) and is a syncretism of Judeo-Christian and Indo-Iranian doctrines. It was primarily based in Babylon and Persia but spread into China, Tibet, the Roman Empire, and Egypt. It was known as the Religion of Light.

Manichaeism was a religion of ultimate dualism; everything spiritual was good, and everything material was evil with certain objects and activities being more evil than others were. For example, to be good, one must abstain from meat, wine, and sexual intercourse. Manichaeism promoted the concept that sexual desire and intercourse were evil, in and of themselves, even within marriage. Procreation was particularly evil because, through procreation, particles of light (spiritual essence) was enslaved and shrouded in physical matter. Thus, that which is evil captivates that which is good. Of course, this is completely unbiblical and non-Jewish. God created the world, looked at it, and said that it was good, not evil, commanding man to procreate, filling the earth (Genesis 1).

Gnosticism too shared this demonically inspired dualistic philosophy of life. They believed that matter was essentially evil and only that which is pure spirit is sinless. They stressed esoteric, spiritual knowledge as the way of salvation, rejecting the incarnation of Christ and faith in Him as the means of salvation. Because of this compartmentalization of existence, the spirit being separate from the flesh, many Gnostics believed that they could be spiritual and yet wholly given over to immoral lifestyles. On the other hand, some Gnostics were driven to asceticism and even masochism because of their belief that all matter and flesh is evil.

How does this relate to marriage, divorce, and remarriage? These unbiblical demonic influences in the early church resulted in an increasingly predominant belief that sexual intercourse was evil, in and of itself, even within marriage. This promoted an attitude of dishonor towards marriage and an undue exaltation of celibacy among the Church Fathers.

Tertullian and Ambrose both expressed that they preferred the extinction of the human race, to its continuance through procreation. Tertullian even claimed that marriage and adultery were not intrinsically different, but only in the degree of their illegitimacy. Saint Augustine believed that the sexual act in marriage was not sinful, but the passion that accompanies it is. Thus continence in marriage was preferred. Saint Augustine was obviously influenced by being a Manichaen before his conversion to Christianity. Because the church had rejected its Jewish heritage, Manichaeism and Platonic thought both significantly influenced Augustine's beliefs even after conversion.

Albertus and Aquinas believed that sexual intercourse subordinated reason to passion, thus revealing their underlying assumption that passion is evil and sexual intercourse should thus be abstained from. Origen had himself castrated before being ordained, taking Matthew 19:12 literally, that *"there are eunuchs who have made themselves eunuchs for the kingdom of heaven's sake" (NKJV)*. He did this even though Deuteronomy 23:1 says, *"He who is emasculated by crushing or mutilation shall not enter the assembly of the LORD" (NKJV)*, obviously not taking into consideration Christianity's Jewish heritage.

Gregory the Great believed that whenever a married couple engages in sexual intercourse for pleasure, their pleasure pollutes their sexual act. These false beliefs and errant attitudes, coupled with a tragic misunderstanding of Jesus' words concerning the bill of divorce and His and Paul's affirmation of celibacy, were the foundation of an unbiblical and unhealthy worldview that gave rise to the traditional doctrine of divorce.

The foundational concepts of the traditional doctrine of marriage and divorce were clearly expressed in the sixteenth century at the Counsel of Trent (AD 1546–1565). At that time marriage was affirmed to be a sacrament, under the auspices (authority and control) of the Church, and, once solemnized (performed with formal religious rites) indissoluble until death. This affirmation has a nice ring of "truth" to it, but poses three false concepts; that marriage is a sacrament, under ecclesiastical authority, and indissoluble. If these three elements of the traditional doctrine of marriage and divorce are false, then all of the teaching and biblical interpretation based on them has a high probability of containing significant error also. In the following chapters, we will closely examine each of these premises.

# Chapter V
# SACRAMENT OR COVENANT

Just one degree off in orbital calculations can cause a satellite to be totally useless in purpose or lead to its destruction. A seemingly small and insignificant error at the beginning of the solution to a mathematical problem can lead to a large error in the results. A marksman makes sure that his sights are calibrated true; if they are not, the farther he is from a target, the greater the possibility that he will completely miss the mark. In this same way, a slight deviation from truth in Christian doctrine has the potential to lead to devastating consequences in the lives of people.

A foundational teaching of the traditional doctrine of divorce is that marriage is a sacrament. Marriage is the legal and social union of a man and woman in an interdependent familial relationship established by the contractual exchange of relational vows—a marriage covenant. But is marriage a *sacrament*?

A sacrament is *"a formal religious act that is sacred as a sign or symbol of a spiritual reality; especially one believed to have been instituted or recognized by Jesus Christ."*[12] A sacrament is a means of grace; it is a conduit of the spiritual blessing and empowerment of God. Sacraments are administered by, to, in, and for the church. Unbelievers are naturally excluded from the blessing and empowerment of Christian sacraments by a lack of faith. Sacraments are made effective by faith. Without faith, sacraments are powerless and effect no positive change in the unbeliever.

***Baptism*** is a sacrament. It is a formal Christian religious act that is a sign and symbol of a spiritual reality—the believer's death to his former way of life and the beginning of a new life in Christ (Romans 6: 1-14). Baptism was recognized and instructed by Christ for all believers (Matthew 28:19). It is a means of grace for the believer. Through baptism, the believer receives a spiritual cleansing of the soul and deliverance from demonic spiritual strongholds (Acts 2:38). Non-believers may be baptized in water, but all that happens to them is that they get wet; no spiritual grace is imparted because they have not taken the first step in receiving the Spirit of Christ and being born-again!

*Communion*, the Eucharist, is a sacrament, a means of grace for the believer. It is a uniquely Christian formal religious act that was instituted by Jesus and is a sign of His sacrificial death on the cross (Matthew 26:26-29). Through communion, the believer regularly receives the soul cleansing power inherent in the blood of Christ. Physical and emotional healing grace is also imparted for the ones who believe that by His stripes, we are healed (I Peter 2:24). For the believer, in a real and meaningful way, communion is a means of personally encountering Jesus Christ. For non-believers, communion is not a means of the grace of God, though they partake of the elements. Non-believers do not encounter Jesus, whom they do not believe in.

A side note concerning the Eucharist—I do not understand the Protestant tradition of not making the Eucharist at least a weekly part of corporate worship. Perhaps it is a reaction to the Catholic and Eastern Orthodox doctrine of transubstantiation, that the elements of the Eucharist miraculously change into the actual blood and body of Christ while keeping only the appearance of bread and wine. But the way to overcome perceived errant doctrine is through teaching the truth, not by *limiting* the practice of the sacrament.

Some argue that they intend to keep the Eucharist special by only partaking of it monthly or a few times a year. If that argument is applied to other elements of the Christian faith then church attendance, worship, prayer, and bible study should also be limited, in order to keep them special (of course I speak sarcastically). If the Eucharist is a vital means of grace for the believer, one uniquely instituted by Christ, then it would only seem logical that we would partake of the elements at every available opportunity.

The Eucharist is special enough, in and of itself. It is the only means of worship and grace that is unique to the Christian faith! Other "faiths" pray, worship, regularly meet, and even perform water baptisms, but no others have the Eucharist. No other religion has Jesus or embraces his sacrificial death on the cross, the passion of Christ. Could it be that there are those who are sick and weak among us, spiritually, emotionally, and physically, because we do not at least weekly avail ourselves of the special grace, the forgiveness and power for life that is released through the Eucharist?

Back to the subject at hand, Baptism and the Eucharist are readily understood as sacraments throughout Christendom and even among non-believers. However, marriage in no way fits the definition of a sacrament. Marriage is not a formal religious act; it is a legal and social union of a man and woman creating a new family. Furthermore, marriage is an earthly union, one not experienced or continued in heaven. Jesus said that "*When people rise from the dead, they will not marry, nor will they be given to someone to marry*" (Matthew 22:30 NCV). Marriage ends at death.

Marriage does have significant spiritual ramifications and can be a spiritual experience for those so minded; but it is not, in and of itself, a religious act; and it is certainly not a strictly Christian act. Irreligious, non-spiritually minded couples get married and their marriage covenants are just as binding, meaningful, and real as the marriage covenants of Christian couples! Furthermore, the marriage ceremony performed by an atheistic mayor, judge, or notary public is just as binding before God and as legally enforceable by civil authority as a marriage ceremony performed by a pastor, priest, rabbi, bishop, or the Pope himself!

Unlike the Eucharist, Jesus did not *institute* marriage, as is customary for a sacrament; nor did He command Christians to be married or perform marriage ceremonies like He did with baptism; and marriage was certainly not considered a sacrament in New Testament times. If marriage were a sacrament, then single Christians would be missing out on a spiritual blessing from God and could be considered second rate citizens in the Kingdom of God.

The statement that "marriage is not a sacrament," does not mean that marriage is not important or of value. Marriage is of tremendous importance, socially and spiritually, worthy of respect, and honorable. *"Marriage should be honored by everyone"* (Hebrews 13:4 NCV). To the Christian, marriage can be and should be considered a sacred and holy covenant! But marriage is not a sacrament, as the word "sacrament" is commonly defined and understood throughout Christendom.

So where did the concept of marriage being a sacrament come from? St. Augustine, writing "To Plllentius – On Adulterous Marriages" in AD 419 was one of the earliest of the Church Fathers to argue that marriage was sacramental in nature. However, it was not until AD 1164 that marriage was ecclesiastically declared to be a sacrament in the fourth book of the "Sentences" of Peter Lombard. Biblical scholar Dr. Instone-Brewer notes the following.

> Roman Catholic canon law was based on Augustine, as systematized by Thomas Aquinas in the thirteenth century. Although he faithfully summarized the teaching of Augustine on divorce and remarriage, he did not always share the same emphases, and he did not take into account the more subtle nuances, which were hinted at in, Augustine's later rethinking.
>
> Aquinas built on Augustine's view of marriage as a sacrament. This view was aided by the Vulgate translation of μυστήριον in Ephesians 5:32 as *sacramentum*. Before Aquinas, marriage was not considered as a cause of grace, like the other sacraments, but Aquinas **confirmed the full sacramental character of marriage**. This was the final foundation for understanding marriage to be ontologically indissoluble. From this basis it was possible to state conclusively that any reference to divorce in the NT referred only to separation, and that the freedom of 1 Corinthians 7.15 did not include the freedom to remarry. Separation was 'from bed and board' (*a mensa et thoro*) but not the end of the marriage.[13] (emphasis mine)

Marriage being declared a sacrament was incorrectly founded upon the Latin translation of the Greek word μυστήριον, **mustēriŏn**, *moos-tay´-ree-on*, in Ephesians 5:32 as *sacramentum*. In the following quote of Ephesians 5:28-33 (NKJV), the English translation of **mustēriŏn** is the word, "mystery."

*So husbands ought to love their own wives as their own bodies; he who loves his wife loves himself. For no one ever hated his own flesh, but nourishes and cherishes it, just as the Lord does the church. For we are members of His body, of His flesh and of His bones. "For this reason a man shall leave his father and mother and be joined to his wife, and the two shall become one flesh." This is a great **MYSTERY**, but I speak concerning Christ and the church. Nevertheless let each one of you in particular so love his own wife as himself, and let the wife see that she respects her husband.* (emphasis mine)

**Mustēriŏn** means "a religious secret, secret rite, secret teaching, or mystery"[14]. It does not mean "sacrament." Furthermore, not only does **mustēriŏn** not mean "sacrament," but in this passage, **mustēriŏn**, "mystery," does not even refer to marriage; it refers to the relationship between Christ and the church. This relationship was a revelation that Paul received, was excited about, and shared in several places in his epistles.

Some argue that marriage should be considered a sacrament because it is a sign and symbol of the relationship between Jesus and the church, an important spiritual reality. Is marriage a **sign or symbol** of Jesus' relationship with the church? No, it is a metaphor of that relationship. Marriage is an earthly union that is used to help us understand a spiritual reality. A "sign" points to something; whereas a metaphor is a figure of speech which highlights conceptual similarities. Adultery, divorce, farming, fishing, and shepherding are also biblical metaphors used to explain spiritual realities. Should fishing be considered a sacrament? I wish fishing were a sacrament; I would make every effort to do so regularly!

Just because marriage is used as a means of illustrating the organic and personal relationship between Jesus and the church, does not mean that marriage should be considered a sacrament. Reformation theology rejected this concept. Martin Luther stated that "marriage is a worldly thing"[15] and did not believe that marriage was a sacrament. The Puritans also rejected the concept of marriage being a sacrament. They strongly affirmed that marriage is covenantal in nature; and of course, Puritan doctrine had a significant influence in the founding of the government and social order of the United States of America.

Marriage does not even remotely fit the definition of a sacrament. Jesus reprimanded the Pharisees for declaring that one vow was more binding than another was (Matthew 5:33-37). Through this, He taught that we should be people of integrity, people of our word. Inspiring and enabling individuals to be people of integrity at heart, people whose word is their bond, keeping their vows, covenants, and contracts will make marriages stronger. Declaring marriage a sacrament does not make the marriage bond stronger. It only enables the bishopric, church leadership, to usurp civil authority and extend and impose their rule over people's lives, enforcing the errant doctrine of the indissolubility of marriage! Enforcing the doctrine of the indissolubility of marriage was the ultimate reason marriage was declared to be a sacrament. But does the church have authority to establish or enforce such an edict? Civil verses ecclesiastical authority over marriage and divorce will be discussed in-depth in the next chapter.

After declaring marriage a sacrament and indissoluble, the bishopric reinterpreted biblical passages concerning divorce to fit their doctrine, declaring that such passages did not refer to divorce, but only referred to separation from room and board. Rather than studying the text to understand what the author meant, one reads into the text a translation that fits his ideology. The fact that marriage is not a sacrament but is a covenant is an important foundational element of developing a biblical doctrine of marriage, divorce, and remarriage!

# Chapter VI
# ECCLESIASTICAL OR CIVIL

God is the supreme authority over everything and everyone. As Christians, we accept this as true, and yet God created man with the power of choice and has delegated specific authority to mankind. In doing so, God also established social authority structures, human institutions, as a means of establishing and maintaining personal, domestic, social, and religious order. For example, God established the family and has delegated appropriate domestic authority and corresponding responsibility to the parents. The fifth of the Ten Commandments is *"Honor your father and mother. Then you will live a long, full life in the land the LORD your God will give you"* (Exodus 20:12 NLT).

In the first century, God established the church and delegated it authority in order to accomplish its purposes and responsibilities. Jesus gave the church: Apostles, prophets, evangelists, pastors, and teachers.

> *Their responsibility is to equip God's people to do his work and build up the church, the body of Christ, until we come to such unity in our faith and knowledge of God's Son that we will be mature and full grown in the Lord, measuring up to the full stature of Christ* (Ephesians 4:11-13 NLT).

God also establishes civil governments (local, regional, national, and international) and has delegated specific authority to them.

> *Let every person be subject to the governing authorities; for there is no authority except from God, and <u>those authorities</u>*

*that exist have been instituted by God. Therefore whoever*
*resists authority resists what God has appointed, and those*
*who resist will incur judgment. For rulers are not a terror*
*to good conduct, but to bad. Do you wish to have no fear of*
*the authority? Then do what is good, and you will receive its*
*approval; for it is God's servant for your good. But if you do*
*what is wrong, you should be afraid, for the authority does*
*not bear the sword in vain! It is the servant of God to execute*
*wrath on the wrongdoer* (Romans 13:1-4 NRSV). (emphasis
mine)

Please note that the above verses were written initially to Christians
in Rome. The Apostle Paul was speaking of the Roman Government, an anti-
Christian, anti-Semitic, pagan government that was in no fashion based upon
the Mosaic Law. Yet Paul affirmed that its authority to rule came from God.
Civil government has been instituted, appointed, and ordained by God to
execute wrath on the wrongdoer.

When challenged about paying taxes, Jesus too affirmed that we are to
submit to the authority of the existing civil government.

*Then the Pharisees met together to think of a way to trap*
*Jesus into saying something for which they could accuse him.*
*They decided to send some of their disciples, along with the*
*supporters of Herod, to ask him this question: "Teacher, we*
*know how honest you are. You teach about the way of God*
*regardless of the consequences. You are impartial and don't*
*play favorites. Now tell us what you think about this: Is it right*
*to pay taxes to the Roman government or not?" But Jesus*
*knew their evil motives. "You hypocrites!" he said. "Whom*
*are you trying to fool with your trick questions? Here, show*
*me the Roman coin used for the tax." When they handed him*
*the coin, he asked, "Whose picture and title are stamped on*
*it?" "Caesar's," they replied. "Well, then," he said, "give to*
*Caesar what belongs to him. But everything that belongs to*
*God must be given to God." His reply amazed them, and they*
*went away* (Matthew 22:15-22 NLT).

In developing a biblical theology of marriage, a fundamental question one MUST answer is "What authority structure should govern issues concerning marriage, divorce, and remarriage?" Are these and related issues under domestic, religious, or civil authority, or a combination thereof? If it is a combination, where does one draw the lines of authority and responsibility?

It is commonly assumed by Christians that the church has been given the authority and responsibility to declare who can or cannot get married, who can or cannot get a divorce, which divorcées can or cannot get married, and what marriages are or are not recognized by God. Does the church have this responsibility and the corresponding necessary authority and power to enforce its judgements?

Moses established both civil and religious authority structures for the nation of Israel. He also gave instructions concerning domestic issues. Apparently, most issues concerning marriage, divorce, and remarriage fell under domestic authority. Marriages were primarily a familial affair with little civil or religious oversight. Even the "*get*," the Jewish bill of divorce, originally, was a relatively private domestic affair only requiring the husband to write the document and give it to his wife (Deuteronomy 24:1). This was similar to several Arabic countries today, where a man may divorce his wife with no civil intervention or oversight.

Moses did establish a few limited civil laws concerning marriage, divorce, and remarriage. He also clearly instructed that difficult issues and heated domestic disagreements be brought before the civil authorities. For example, concerning a case of marriage and divorce for a specific immoral reason, Deuteronomy 22:13-19 says:

> *Suppose a man marries a woman and, after sleeping with her, changes his mind about her and falsely accuses her of having slept with another man. He might say, 'I discovered she was not a virgin when I married her.' If the man does this, the woman's father and mother must bring the proof of her virginity to the **leaders of the town**. Her father must tell them, 'I gave my daughter to this man to be his wife, and now he has turned against her. He has accused her of shameful things, claiming that she was not a virgin when he married her. But here is the proof of my daughter's virginity.' Then they must spread the*

*cloth before the **judges**. The **judges** must then punish the man.
They will fine him one hundred pieces of silver, for he falsely
accused a virgin of Israel. The payment will be made to the
woman's father. The woman will then remain the man's wife,
**and he may never divorce her*** (NLT). (emphasis mine)

These judges were civic leaders appointed by a consensus of the
people. These judges were not priests; they were respected members of the
community. Deuteronomy 16:18-20 says,

*Appoint judges and officials for each of your tribes in all the
towns the L ORD your God is giving you. They will judge the
people fairly throughout the land. You must never twist justice
or show partiality. Never accept a bribe, for bribes blind the
eyes of the wise and corrupt the decisions of the godly. Let
true justice prevail, so you may live and occupy the land that
the L ORD your God is giving you* (NLT). (emphasis mine)

From this and other similar passages, one can readily deduce that in
Israel, issues concerning marriage and divorce were subject to civil authority,
not religious. Of course, in Moses' day and culture, as in our day and culture,
some people served simultaneously in domestic, civil, and religious positions
of authority. However, although a person serves as a leader in his family,
church, and civil government, each role contains specific responsibilities and
authority.

There was one specific case concerning marriage that required the
involvement of the priesthood—the law of jealousy (Numbers 5:11-31). If a
man suspected his wife of adultery, but had no witnesses, he could bring her
to a priest in the tabernacle who would perform a grain sacrifice on her behalf,
mix water with dust from the tabernacle floor, have the woman repeat a curse
and drink the "bitter water." If she were guilty, she would be barren, waste
away from sickness, and become an outcast among her people. If she were
not guilty, she would be fine, and thus allay the unfounded jealousy of her
husband.

Although this law of jealousy concerned a married couple, it in no way regulated marriage, divorce, or remarriage or gave the priesthood authority to do so. If the wife was innocent of the charge of adultery, the purpose of the ceremony was to break a jealous spirit in the husband that could destroy the marriage, thus being a support to marriage, and not legislation over marriage. If the wife were guilty, this ceremony would uncover her wickedness, but did not actuate a divorce. Also note that this trial was not like pagan "trials by fire" in which it took a miracle to survive the ordeal, being guilty until proven innocent miraculously. In this "trial," it took supernatural intervention for the woman to be subjected to the curse, being innocent until proven guilty supernaturally.

In its article on "Marriage," the *Encyclopedia of the Early Church* notes that "In the course of the first centuries, the church became increasingly aware that marriage though regulated by civil rules, had a Christian meaning for the baptized. In the eleventh and twelfth centuries, the church attributed complete jurisdiction to itself ".[16] (emphasis mine) In other words, the church took authority from the civil government that it previously did not have. This authority or jurisdiction was not given by God, but was unjustly taken, usurped by the church and has caused problems ever since! Authority unjustly taken will not last and has no power to enforce its will.

For a relatively brief period of time and for a minute percentage of the world's population, the Roman Catholic Church usurped civil authority concerning marriage and divorce in Europe. However, today in America and in countries around the world, the church has not been able to maintain such authority and only imposes its will concerning marriage, divorce, and remarriage through manipulation and coercion. The church does and should influence civil policy, but the church does not, in and of itself, possess civil authority. Civil governments have been ordained by God to have jurisdiction over issues concerning marriage and divorce, not the church!

The Puritans vehemently opposed the doctrine of marriage being a sacrament or in any way under ecclesiastical authority. They taught that marriage was a covenant and under civil authority. The Puritans went so far in opposing the Church of England on this point that, for a few years, they actually refused to submit to English civil legislation that an Anglican Priest or Bishop perform marriages. Instead, they performed marriage ceremonies in town halls presided over by a locally appointed civil, non-ecclesiastical authority.

By the way, the Puritans were not very puritanical, as that word is used today. Puritanical means to have a rigid morality, a strictness and austerity in regards to religion and conduct. As commonly used, it also often implies a separatist, exclusionary, prideful, holier-than-thou attitude. Unlike this, the Puritans were, for their day, a very practical, earthy, humble people, having many beliefs that were anti-traditional and counter-cultural, directly opposing the beliefs of the established church.

They had a strong work ethic that resulted in financial prosperity, countering religious asceticism and vows of poverty. Their views concerning ecclesiastical authority were practical, limiting the authority of the church to religious matters. The Puritan's beliefs concerning sexual intercourse were opposite of the prevailing beliefs of the church, Roman Catholic and Anglican. They opposed the concept that sexual intercourse, in and of itself, was evil, teaching that sexual intercourse was not only acceptable and proper within marriage, but that it was a blessing from God to be fully enjoyed with great passion.

Furthermore, Puritan pastors were outspoken against the doctrine of priestly celibacy, declaring it heresy, and calling it a doctrine of demons! They taught a down-to-earth religion, one that effected every aspect of their lives. They were called Puritans, because they opposed the hypocrisy of the leadership of the established church and their anti-biblical doctrines. Hoping to change the church from within, they were unlike the Separatists who believed that the established church was beyond hope and thus separated from the Church of England. Leland Ryken wrote a very good book about the Puritans entitled, *Worldly Saints*[17]. It covers this information in detail.

The founding fathers of the United States of America chose to establish our civil government based upon a synthesis of biblical principles, English parliamentary procedures, and Puritan doctrine and philosophy. In doing so, issues concerning marriage and divorce were and are considered civil matters— not religious. Ministers, who perform wedding ceremonies, do so under civil authority, acting as agents of the state. A minister that is not licensed by the state to perform weddings cannot do so legally. In the first century and today, the church has absolutely no legal jurisdiction over marriage, divorce, and remarriage. Biblically, practically, socially, and legally, it is evident that civil government is God's delegated authority over issues concerning marriage, divorce, and remarriage—not the church!

Unfortunately, some ministers that believe the traditional doctrine of divorce actually claim that certain couples, though legally married, are not truly married in the "eyes of God." If this is true, please show me one such biblical case. I do not know of a single example. Some people offer the relationship between Herod and Herodias (Matthew 14:3&4) as an example of a civil marriage that God did not recognize; but a close examination of their relationship actually supports the principal truth that marriage is under civil authority.

John the Baptist declared that Herod's relationship with Herodias, his brother Phillip's wife, was not legal. Was John the Baptist speaking of civil or religious law? The New King James Version says, *"For Herod had laid hold of John and bound him, and put him in prison for the sake of Herodias, his brother **Philip's wife**. Because John had said to him, 'It is **not lawful** for you to have her'" (Matthew 14:3-4).* From Josephus, a first century Jewish Historian, we learn that Herodias left Phillip, her husband, and sent him a letter of separation;[18] but under Jewish **civil law**, Herodias could not **legally** divorce Phillip; only the husband could divorce the wife. Thus, Herodias was still legally bound as a wife to Phillip and could not legally marry Herod. Although Herod treated her as a wife and possibly declared her to be so, their relationship was not a legally recognized marriage according to Jewish civil law. Herodias and Herod were living together in an adulterous relationship because Phillip refused to release Herodias from their marriage covenant. Correctly understanding Herod and Herodias' relationship thus supports the concept that marriage is under civil authority.

Please note that several modern translations incorrectly interpret this passage in such a way as to indicate that Herodias was Herod's wife and was no longer Phillip's wife. For example, the New Living Translation states, *"For*

*Herod had arrested and imprisoned John as a favor to **his wife** Herodias (**the former wife of Herod's brother Philip)*"* (Matthew 14:3). (emphasis mine) The New Century Version also incorrectly translates it as follows, *"Sometime before this, Herod had arrested John, tied him up, and put him into prison. Herod did this because of Herodias, who **had been the wife of Philip**, Herod's brother. John had been telling Herod, 'It is not lawful for you **to be married** to Herodias'"* (Matthew 14:3&4). (emphasis mine)

Both the New Living Translation and the New Century Version incorrectly imply that Herodias divorced Phillip and married Herod. The Greek, however, supports the more wooden and literal New King James Version, as opposed to the more dynamic versions. When we examine Jesus' words concerning divorce, similar errant assumptions are made by the more dynamic translations.

Which authority structure, domestic, civil, or ecclesiastical, is to govern marital issues? This is an important principal truth that one must wrestle through in establishing a biblical theology of marriage. Not only are there no examples of legally sanctioned marriages that God did not recognize, but God recognized and even blessed marriages that were extremely outside of the clear boundaries of the divine ideal and even the Mosaic Law, but legal under the existing domestic and civil authority structures.

Jacob married two women (sisters in fact) and had children with them both and their two maids (Genesis 35:22-26). God clearly recognized and even blessed these relationships, even though marrying sisters was later outlawed in the Mosaic Law (Leviticus 18:18). Jacob favored one wife over the other, and her two sons over the other ten sons. This gave rise to many familial problems. Yet, God blessed this family in continuing the Abrahamic Covenant and Blessing. Their twelve sons ended up fathering the twelve tribes of Israel.

King David was a polygamist and even initiated an adulterous relationship with Bathsheba, resulting in her becoming pregnant while Uriah, her husband, was away at war. David desperately tried to cover his sin. He went so far as to have Uriah killed and then marrying Bathsheba. Due to David's sin, the child died and violence plagued David's family for generations. However, God not only recognized the marriage between David and Bathsheba, but even continued the rule of Israel through another son of their union, Solomon (II Samuel 11 & 12); and it is significant to note that Solomon was God's choice, not David's!

It is possible that Solomon faced many challenges growing up due to being the child of such a scandalous relationship. He could have been thought of negatively by the community at large and even ostracized by his own family members, especially by his older brothers who were jockeying for position to become the next King of Israel. These challenges could have prepared him to be a much better king than David's other more "legitimate" sons. No one really knows, but this would fit God's pattern of training his chosen ones for leadership through much adversity. It would also help us understand Solomon's lack of self-confidence when he was chosen to be King. God's ways are certainly far beyond ours!

Solomon ended up having 700 wives and 300 concubines (I Kings 11:1-7) although having that many wives was clearly against the Mosaic Law *"The king must not take many wives for himself, because they will lead him away from the Lord* (Deuteronomy 17:17 NLT). Not only did Solomon marry many wives, but he also married women from other nations, which was also forbidden by the Law.

> *When the Lord your God hands these nations over to you and you conquer them, you must completely destroy them. Make no treaties with them and show them no mercy. Do not intermarry with them, and don't let your daughters and sons marry their sons and daughters. They will lead your young people away from me to worship other gods. Then the anger of the Lord will burn against you, and he will destroy you* (Deuteronomy 7:2-4 NLT).

Solomon married many women from other nations; and just as was predicted, his heart turned away from the One True God to worshipping false gods. The commandment to not do something implies that it is possible for the person to do it, although they shouldn't. Breaking law, whether natural, civil, or spiritual, results in negative consequences. In this case, although Solomon broke the Law of Moses by marrying many foreign women, he was still married to these women, being legally and relationally bound to them. The spiritual consequence of Solomon breaking the Law was his heart turning further away from following the One True God to following after idols. This resulted in the downfall of his kingdom.

In the New Testament, Jesus said to the woman at the well, *'You're right! You don't have a husband—for you have had five husbands, and you aren't even married to the man you're living with now'"* (John 4:17-18 NLT). Jesus, God in the flesh, recognized all five of her previous marriages. Also notice that Jesus drew a clear distinction between her five previous husbands and the man she was living with—an unlawful relationship (fornication).

These are just a few of the many examples of marriages that God recognized though they clearly did not fit the divine ideal and were even in violation of the Law of Moses. Of course, concerning intimate relationships, the further a person moves away from the divine ideal, the more problems a person will have. The laws and principles of God are meant *for* our good, not to keep us *from* good!

Does the civil government have the authority to declare who is to be recognized as a Christian and who is not? Can it legislate who can receive communion or baptism? Of course not! Then why would we think that the church has the authority or responsibility to declare who may get married, divorced, or remarried, and who may not? If the government assumed authority in matters of faith, would people be bound before God to accept it? No! But Christian leaders around the world who accept as truth the traditional doctrine of divorce have assumed authority that they clearly do not have—that of declaring who can marry and who cannot!

Now let us address the other extreme; for various reasons, some Christian couples choose to live together as husband and wife, though they are not legally married. Some go as far as to have a religious wedding service presided over by a minister or priest, and publicly declare their vows. They do this without obtaining marriage licenses. If one accepts that the civil government is God's delegated authority over issues concerning marriage and divorce, can a couple be married in the "eyes of God" without proper civil recognition of the union? No, they cannot.

Some might argue that marriage predates civil government. This is true, but that was before God instituted civil governments and delegated appropriate authority to them. As Christians we are to obey civil authorities as long as it does not contradict our religious convictions. Our place is to do what we can to influence civil governments to enact and enforce righteous laws. In no way can we impose or enforce laws or judgements of a civil nature apart from proper governmental procedure and authority.

It is important to recognize that the church does not have jurisdiction over marriage, divorce, and remarriage. Since the church does not have the authority to declare the viability of marriages, the traditional doctrine of divorce is mute and powerless! It is mute in that it cannot speak authoritatively on this issue. It is powerless in that it cannot force couples to stay together who wish to divorce, demand couples to divorce who wish to remain married, or direct divorcées to not marry again!

One cannot emphasize strongly enough the biblical truth, fact, and reality that issues concerning marriage, divorce, and remarriage are under civil authority and not under ecclesiastical authority! The traditional doctrine of divorce is founded upon the belief, the assumption, the premise that issues concerning marriage and divorce are under the auspices of the church, but biblically and legally such issues are under the jurisdiction of civil government and NOT the church. Therefore, Christians (clergy or laity) have no right, authority, or responsibility to declare a couple married or divorced in the eyes of God or man, apart from proper delegated civil authority!

Practically speaking, marriage and divorce issues need to be under civil authority. The primary responsibility of civil government is to establish and maintain order in society. Punishment of evildoers is a primary means of fulfilling this mandate. Men and women that abuse, neglect, or abandon their spouses and/or children need to be held accountable and punished for their actions. The weak and disenfranchised of society need the protection provided by civil government. The church does not have the authority or responsibility to punish evildoers in society, especially those who are not members of the church.

Although the church does not have direct authority over issues concerning marriage, one of its primary responsibilities is to equip people to serve in positions of leadership in civil government. Through these leaders, righteous laws are created and enforced. The Bible says, *"When the righteous are in authority, the people rejoice; But when a wicked man rules, the people groan"* (Proverbs 29:2 NKJV).

Another errant concept that permeates American society is the concept that "civil government does not have the right to legislate morality." Usually the person stating this argument is referencing sexual immorality. To legislate means to make or enact laws. Morality is a system of moral conduct. Moral conduct is right and wrong behavior. Therefore, what they are saying is that "civil government does not have the right or authority to enact laws concerning right and wrong behavior." That is obviously wrong. The truth is that the primary job of the civil government, as ordained by God, is to legislate morality, to make and enact laws concerning right and wrong behavior. This includes sexual morality! Even in today's immoral climate, sexual intercourse with children is against the law, rightly so. Polygamy is against the law; and until recently, homosexuality was against the law. Civil government not only has the right to legislate morality, but it has the responsibility to legislate morality, including sexual morality!

Civil government *"is the servant of God to execute wrath on the wrongdoer"* (Romans 13:4 NRSV). It is the civil government's responsibility and duty to punish fornicators, adulterers, homosexuals, thieves, murderers, child abusers, and all other forms of immoral behavior! It is the church's responsibility to empower through prayer, equip through teaching, and disciple through mentoring, civic leaders, enabling them to perform their civic duty to legislate morality.

The truth that issues concerning marriage and divorce being under civil authority and not ecclesiastical authority is an important element of a biblically based theology of marriage. Without the authority to declare who is married and who is not, the church's proper place is a position of support and empowerment—not control! It was by usurping civil authority in these matters that the church of the Dark Ages was able to declare and promote a great deception—the indissolubility marriage.

# Chapter VII
# INDISSOLUBLE OR BREAKABLE

"Indissoluble" means that an object or entity is "incapable of being annulled, undone, decomposed, disintegrated, or broken. It is permanent."[19] Acting under usurped civil authority, *"The Council of Trent in 1564 made the dogma of the indissolubility of marriage a matter of faith. According to Session XXIV, Canon V, 'If anyone shall say that the bond of matrimony can be dissolved for the cause of heresy, or of injury due to cohabitation, or of willful desertion, let him be anathema.'"*[20] In other words, even if a person's spouse is a heretic, abusive, and willfully deserts them, the marriage bond CANNOT be broken; and if anyone teaches that marriage can be broken, he will be cursed by and excommunicated from the Church! This is a sober statement, "authoritatively" establishing marriage as indissoluble and putting the entire weight of the Roman Catholic Church behind it.

The doctrine of the indissoluble nature of marriage arose partially, although not predominantly, from an attempt by the early Church Fathers to interpret (understand, explain, and apply) Jesus' difficult statements concerning divorce in Matthew 5:31 & 32, 19:3-12, Luke 16:18, and Mark 10:2-12.

Frankly, indissolubility is a logical conclusion if you take Jesus' difficult statements at face value **irrespective** of their literary or Near Eastern cultural context. For example, Jesus said *"It was also said, 'Whoever divorces his wife must give her a bill of divorce.' But I say to you, whoever divorces his wife (unless the marriage is unlawful) causes her to commit adultery, and whoever marries a divorced woman commits adultery"* (Matthew 5:31 & 32 NAB).

Upon a cursory observation, this and the other similar verses readily lead one to believe that Jesus purposed to repudiate (reject as invalid) the Mosaic Law concerning divorce. When one considers ONLY Jesus' assertion (as commonly translated) that a divorced woman commits adultery when marrying another man, it is only logical to deduce that Jesus (God in the flesh) did not recognize her divorce as valid. Therefore, though the woman had obtained a legal divorce performed by men, she was actually not divorced and was still married to her first husband "in God's eyes." Thus, marriage is indissoluble.

Furthermore, the only exception to this seems to be if the "marriage" was never a viable marriage to begin with. The phrase "except for fornication" (KJV), or "unless the marriage is unlawful" (NAB) affirms this IF you take the passage at face value as it is interpreted and irrespective of any contextual considerations or other biblical evidence.

In the passages in Matthew 19 and in Mark 10, Jesus also refers His hearers to God's original design for the family, that of the man leaving his father and mother and cleaving to his wife, becoming "one flesh." At face value, this too reinforces the concept that Jesus intended to repudiate the Law of Moses concerning divorce and reinstate marriage being indissoluble as it was in the Garden of Eden. The concept of marriage being indissoluble is further reinforced if one incorrectly interprets "becoming one flesh" as "becoming like one person." As discussed earlier, this phrase incorrectly leads one to believe that the couple experiences some type of metaphysical metamorphosis that permanently joins them together as a single entity.

It has been said that a "Text" without a "Context" is a "Pretext"–an assumed interpretation that often hides the author's intended meaning. A contextually based interpretation of these difficult passages yields a completely different message than a cursory, "plain" or straightforward interpretation. The context of these passages will be discussed in detail in later chapters. For now, it is sufficient to examine just one element of the literary context of the passages in Matthew 19 and Mark 10 that negates the belief that marriage is indissoluble, or that Jesus intended to assert that marriage is indissoluble.

In the Matthew 19 and Mark 10 passages, Jesus' own words directly imply that marriage is breakable—not indissoluble! Unfortunately, many times when sharing this concept, people "assume" that I wish to assert that marriage should be considered "disposable"–something lightly entered and easily broken. Please do not misunderstand me; in no way am I proposing that marriage is "*disposable*" or should be considered so! "*Disposable*" implies that something is of little value and can be discarded at will once it has lost its usefulness or once it no longer fulfills its intended purpose. Marriage is too important to be considered so. Marriage and family is the foundation of social structure. Dysfunctional and broken marriages have the potential of resulting in generations of dysfunctional and broken people. We should never consider marriage "*disposable.*"

However, we should recognize that marriage is "breakable" and treat it accordingly. One handles a priceless and fragile China vase much differently than a common cast-iron pot. The more fragile and valuable an item, the greater care with which it is handled! In like manner, it would be a positive step for every married couple and for every culture to recognize that marriage is breakable and work together to strengthen and defend marriages. Like a China vase, marriage is both priceless and fragile, and it should be cared for and protected with passionate diligence.

Jesus' command concerning marriage **plainly infers** that marriage is breakable and not indissoluble. Jesus said "*What God has joined together, let not man separate*" (Matthew 19:6 NKJV). "*let not separate*" in Greek is "μή-χωρίζετω, (may-kho-rid-ze-to)." "Χωρίζω (kho-rid'-zo)*"* means to place room between, put apart, or separate. It is significant that the participle "μη (may)" is used instead of "οὐχ (ook)" or "οὐ μη (oo may)." "Οὐ (oo)" is commonly used as an absolute negative or absolute denial as in "never" or "cannot;" and "οὐ μη (oo may)" is a negation of double emphasis and strength.

Unlike double negatives in proper English that cancel each other and actually affirm the positive, a double negative in Greek is used to emphasize the negative aspect of the subject at hand. This is similar to the use of double negatives in common English. For example, "Ain't no way," is an emphatic statement of double negative emphasis meaning, "there is *absolutely* no way."

Conversely, "μη *(may),*" as used in Matthew 19:6, is a primary participle of **qualified negation** as in "should not" or "let not." In other words, mankind **should not** separate what God has joined together. This directly implies that mankind has the potential of separating what God has joined together, not that it is impossible for them to do so. Thus marriage is NOT indissoluble and can be broken by man's action, although he shouldn't. Therefore, the command of Jesus concerning divorce actually precludes one from accepting the assertion that Jesus intended to affirm or endorse, much less legislate, that marriage is indissoluble!

People *can* break their marriage unions. They should not, but they have the *potential* of doing so. The Bible commands mankind not to commit murder. Why, because we have the potential of committing murder. In the same way mankind has the potential of cutting their marital bonds through divorce. In a real way, death is similar to divorce. In death there is a separation between body and soul. In divorce there is a separation between husband and wife, a breaking of the marital bond. Believing that marriage is indissoluble is just as senseless as believing that man is immortal and cannot be killed.

In the Garden of Eden, man was immortal; and in heaven, man will be immortal once again. However, from the time of man's expulsion from the Garden until Christ returns at the end of this age, mankind is mortal and will suffer death–a separation of body and soul. In like manner, in the Garden of Eden, marriage was indissoluble, being the *perfect* union, of two *perfect* people, for eternity. Today, however, marriage is neither indissoluble, nor eternal. Because of sin, marriage is now the temporal, *imperfect* union, of two *imperfect* people that ends in either death or, possibly and far too often, in divorce–the death of the marriage union!

The command in Deuteronomy 24:4 not to remarry a former spouse that has married another and subsequently been divorced again or widowed, also reveals that marriage is not indissoluble. Many years ago this was the key verse that the Holy Spirit used to teach me that the traditional doctrine of the indissolubility of marriage is erroneous. If the marriage union were unbreakable, remarrying the first spouse would be the logical thing for a person to do regardless of any intervening adulterous and illegitimate marriages.

Today, based on the doctrine of the indissolubility of marriage, some pastors and priests actually counsel people to divorce their current spouse and remarry their first spouse because they are still married "in the sight of God" to their first spouse. This counsel is completely unscriptural and outside the boundaries of common sense!

It has been said that it takes two to break a marriage, but the truth is that it only takes one! Any marriage can end in divorce if a person hardens his heart against his spouse, regardless of how loving and forgiving his spouse is. Even God, the perfect husband, suffered divorce when His spouse, Israel hardened her heart against Him.

Fact: marriage can be broken through divorce; and the doctrine of the indissolubility of marriage is false! The truth is that a legal divorce terminates, dissolves, and breaks the marriage union. Marriage is not indissoluble, but is breakable and should be understood and treated as such. This is a big pill for some people to swallow, but it is the truth; and if ingested it will foster increasing health in individuals, marriages, families, the church, and society at large!

# Chapter VIII
# CIVIL LAW DESIGNED BY GOD

### DANNY

Danny is over forty and single, having never married. Over the years, he has wrestled with the idea of dating and possibly marrying a divorcée. He loves the Lord and would be a good husband and a wonderful father—biological or stepfather. It is sad that the church has hindered this by saying that he cannot rightfully marry a divorcée. With all the fatherless children in our society, how can we deny a brother the honor and privilege of helping to meet such a tremendous need?

Danny, the good news is that God understands your need for companionship, and your desire to be a father. You need not limit your options in seeking a wife to only women that have never been married. You are free to marry a divorcée in the Lord as you will, and as the Lord provides. The question is, "Are you willing to be like God and adopt children, not your own?" (Ephesians 1:5)

Marriage is a legal covenant, *not* a sacrament. Marriage is under civil authority, *not* ecclesiastical. Marriage is breakable, *not* indissoluble. These three premises form the foundation for a renewed biblically based theology of marriage, divorce and remarriage. The foundational scriptures that have been used to support the traditional doctrine of marriage and divorce are the ones where Jesus briefly speaks concerning divorce. Before we examine them, though, it is important to understand related passages in the Law of Moses. These form the foundation for understanding what Jesus said.

Many would classify Moses' day as barbaric. Imagine hundreds of thousands of ex-slaves living in the wilderness with virtually no established civil or religious authority structures or laws. The only civil authority the Israelites had known for four hundred years was that of their slave masters–the Egyptians. Concerning religious authority, the golden calf incident reveals that their religious beliefs had significantly mingled with those of the Egyptians (Deuteronomy 9:6-29) and that they were in desperate need of divine revelation if they were to fulfill the covenant that God had made with their forefathers, Abraham, Isaac, and Jacob.

After God delivered Israel from slavery in Egypt, they went, by God's supernatural guidance in the form of a cloud by day and a pillar of fire by night, to Mount Sinai to receive His Law. Moses ascended the mountain and was gone for forty days without anything to eat or drink. During that time, the people came to believe that Moses was dead, and thus his wishes and leadership did not restrict them. In response to this, they made a golden calf as an idol to worship. The cow was one of the many gods worshiped in Egypt. Upon returning from the mountaintop, Moses found the people worshipping the idol, and except for Moses' intercession, God would have wiped out Israel, then and there.

Moses definitely had his hands full maintaining order, and establishing religious and civil law and authority structures for the new nation of Israel, much less facilitating the radical paradigm changes required by the giving of the Law of Moses. Law, inspired by God, was to be the foundation of man's government, rather than man governing man in the form of a dictatorship–civil, domestic, or religious! It is in this context that Moses wrote down God's teachings on the best way to conduct life.

Many of the teachings of Moses brought significant positive social reform in the treatment of disenfranchised segments of society, especially women, children, slaves, and aliens (as in foreigners, not extraterrestrials). In fact, most of the laws concerning marriage, divorce, and remarriage are for the protection of women. In Moses' day, the legal and social standing of women was drastically lower than that of men. Women had few rights except those given them by their closest male relative. In most Ancient Near Eastern

CIVIL LAW DESIGNED BY GOD   97

cultures, women were considered property and almost totally dependent upon their father's, husband's, or owner's good will. This is still prevalent today in some of the Muslim countries of the Near East.

In his book *Divorce and Remarriage in the Bible*, Dr. David Instone-Brewer highlights the similarities between the Old Testament Israeli culture and other ancient Near Eastern cultures. He writes the following:

> Comparisons of the Pentateuch with other ancient Near Eastern sources have shown that they share the same culture with regard to marriage, divorce and remarriage. Their customs, terminology and laws are similar in almost all respects. ... Because of the similarity of the Pentateuch with other ancient Near Eastern law codes, **we must assume that where the Old Testament is silent, there was a broad agreement with the prevailing culture.** However, the Israelites were very proud that they did not conform to the prevailing culture of the nations surrounding them. **We can therefore assume that when there was a distinctiveness between the Israelites and their neighbors, this would be likely to be recorded in the Pentateuch.** One of the purposes of the Pentateuchal Law was to highlight these differences. [21] (emphasis mine)

During biblical times, in the Near East, when a man desired to marry, he, his father, or a representative would approach the father of the woman that the man wished to marry and establish a marriage covenant. This usually involved the payment of the *mohar*, **the bride price**, which was about ten months wages. It might appear or sound like the groom was purchasing a wife, but it was customary for the bride's father to add his daughter's share of the family inheritance to the *mohar*. The total sum was called the *ketubah*, **the dowry**. At the wedding, the dowry was then given to the bride and groom and could be invested or kept in safekeeping. Technically, the dowry or its equivalent value was considered the bride's property throughout the marriage and the husband was charged with its safekeeping.

These ritual payments served several vital purposes. *First*, they served as the legal seal of the marriage covenant. When money or material wealth changed hands, the marriage covenant was ratified, thus allowing for civil judicial intervention if needed. *Second*, the dowry served as a stable financial foundation for the new family. Several months wages was a significant amount of money for the groom to save up for the *mohar*—the bride price. The groom must prove able and willing to provide for a family. Furthermore, this helped ensure that a marriage covenant was not lightly entered. *Third*, the dowry served as financial security for the wife in case of divorce or the death of her husband; and *fourth*, it served as a significant deterrent to divorce. Dr. Instone-Brewer points out the following:

> The whole system of payments was weighted against divorce, because whoever caused the divorce was penalized financially. If the husband divorced his wife without cause, he usually returned the dowry, and if the wife divorced her husband without cause, she lost her right to some or all of her dowry. However, if the divorce was caused by one partner breaking a stipulation in the marriage contract, the guilty partner was deemed to have caused the divorce and the innocent partner kept the dowry.[22]

Although ancient Near Eastern marriage customs are not specifically delineated in the Pentateuch or the remainder of the Bible, there is much evidence to support that this was the custom in Israel. For example, in Genesis 24, Abraham sent his servant from Canaan back to Abraham's family in Mesopotamia to get a bride for Isaac, his son. The servant took ten camels loaded with much wealth, the bride price that would have made up the first part of the dowry. Likely, Abraham sent an overly large bride price in order to insure the family of Rebekah, the bride-to-be, that she would be well taken care of. He did this because she would be moving a great distance away from her family. We can also assume that Rebekah's father, Bethuel, would have added her share of the family inheritance to the bride price, providing for her an exceptionally large dowry. This helps us understand why Rebekah was so willing to accept the offer of marriage to a man she had never met and to leave her family so quickly. In that culture, security and provision were primary motivations in a woman's selection of a husband.

Another interesting story full of romance, jealousy, deception, and intrigue is found in Genesis 29–31. Abraham's grandson, Jacob, left his family in Canaan to go to Paddan Aram to get a wife from among his mother's relatives. Upon arriving, he met Rachel, his cousin, and fell head-over-heals in love with her. Laban, Rachel's father, made a deal with Jacob for Rachel. In place of a monetary bride price, Jacob agreed to work for Laban for seven years. Considering that the common bride price was about ten months wages, Laban took significant advantage of Jacob and his love for Rachel. At the end of the seven years, Laban took further advantage of Jacob by deceiving him and substituting Leah, Rachel's older, homely sister, for Rachel during the wedding ceremony. Thus Jacob ended up marrying Leah instead of Rachel.

In the morning when Jacob discovered that he had wed Leah, he became angry and challenged Laban. In response, Laban gave a lame excuse about the older daughter needing to marry first. Laban succeeded in his plan of taking advantage of Jacob; and Jacob ended up establishing another marriage covenant to work another seven years for Rachel. He was allowed to consummate his marriage with Rachel only one week after he married Leah, not being required to wait until he paid the full agreed-upon bride price. After fulfilling the bride price stipulations of his second marriage covenant, Jacob continued to work for Laban for six more years in exchange for flocks and herds. God blessed Jacob though, and his flocks and herds multiplied resulting in much of the wealth of Laban's household transferring into Jacob's possession. Laban's sons did not like their father "losing" their inheritance, so they complained to Laban and were likely planning how to cheat Jacob once again.

Jacob heard about this and took note that Laban was not treating him as nicely as he once did. During this period of unrest in Jacob's life, God told him to leave Laban's household and go back to his father's family. He wisely decided to follow God's guidance and take his family back to Canaan where his father and mother lived. He then conspired with Rachel and Leah to leave secretly. They decided to follow him saying,

> *There's nothing left for us to inherit from our father. He treats*
> *us like foreigners and has even cheated us out of* the bride
> price that should have been ours. *Now do whatever God tells*
> *you to do.* Even the property God took from our father and
> gave to you really belongs to us and our children (Genesis
> 31:14-16 CEV). (emphasis mine)

While leaving, Rachel also stole her father's household idols. It was
believed that these idols would protect them from harm, were possibly made
of precious metals and worth a significant amount of money, and possibly also
signified who would inherit the family property. Rachel probably felt justified
in doing this because of the fourteen years of labor that Jacob had given for
her and her sister's bride price. The monetary value of those years of servitude
should have been added to their share of the family inheritance and given to
her and her sister as their dowries. Unfortunately, she was leaving with no
dowry and was thus totally dependent upon Jacob's continued good will.

Another example is found in I Samuel 18 where King Saul required
of David one hundred Philistine foreskins as the bride price for Michal, his
daughter. This was a treacherous plot to have David killed, considering that
he had to kill one hundred or more Philistines in order to take Michal as his
wife. He was required this even though a daughter of Saul had already been
promised to the man who killed Goliath. Going beyond what was required of
him, David killed two hundred Philistines in response to King Saul's gruesome
price.

These are just a few of many such Biblical examples confirming that
the Israelites followed the Near Eastern custom of the bride price and dowry.
As mentioned before, we can assume that where the Pentateuch, the Mosaic
Law, is silent, it was because there was little, if any, difference between the
Hebraic culture and the prevailing culture in the Ancient Near East.

Concerning specific guidelines for marriage, divorce, and remarriage,
relatively little is mentioned in Moses' teachings or the remainder of the
Bible, especially considering the importance of the subject. Moses forbids
sexual intercourse and thus marriage with a close relative (Leviticus 18:6-17),

marrying a woman and her sister (Leviticus 18:18) or a woman and her mother (Leviticus 20:14), and a priest marrying a divorcée or prostitute (Leviticus 21:7). A daughter in line to inherit property was not allowed to marry outside of her tribe (Numbers 36:8); and if a man took a slave girl as his wife and then married another, he was not to diminish the slave wife's food, clothing, or conjugal rights. If he decided to divorce her or refused to meet her needs equitably in comparison to his other wives, she was to be given her freedom at no cost (Exodus 21:10 & 11).

Concerning divorce, a man who rapes a virgin must marry her if her father demands/allows it; and that man is never allowed to divorce her (Deuteronomy 22:29). A man may never divorce his wife whom he wrongfully accused of not being a virgin at the time of their marriage (Deuteronomy 22:19); and a man that divorces his wife may not remarry her if she has subsequently married someone else even though she is widowed or divorced by her second husband (Deuteronomy 24:1-4).

Note the clarity and specificity with which Moses dealt with these issues. Moses does not forbid divorce; nor does he establish guidelines for acceptable or non-acceptable reasons for divorce. One must assume that the common practice of the guilty party in a divorce losing the dowry was sufficient and that Moses, as inspired by God, saw no need for further civil legislation.

Moses clearly does not forbid divorce or a divorcée to marry again. In fact, Deuteronomy 24:1-4 makes provision for a divorcée to remarry legally with no fear of social or legal retribution. Even polygamy was not outlawed; and Exodus 21:10 & 11, Leviticus 18:18, and Leviticus 20:14 all assume that polygamy would continue.

Having briefly reviewed the Ancient Near Eastern and Old Testament biblical culture of marriage, divorce, and remarriage, let us examine closely the passage concerning divorce that Jesus is questioned about in the Gospels by the Pharisees.

Deuteronomy 24: 1-4 (NKJV)
*When a man takes a wife and marries her, and it happens that she finds no favor in his eyes because he has found some uncleanness in her, and he writes her a certificate of divorce,*

*puts it in her hand, and sends her out of his house, when she has departed from his house, and goes and becomes another man's wife, if the latter husband detests her and writes her a certificate of divorce, puts it in her hand, and sends her out of his house, or if the latter husband dies who took her as his wife, then her former husband who divorced her must not take her back to be his wife after she has been defiled; for that is an abomination before the LORD, and you shall not bring sin on the land which the LORD your God is giving you as an inheritance.*

This passage is a prohibition of a man remarrying his ex-wife after she has married another man, regardless of whether her second husband dies or divorces her. One must ask why? **Why would Moses write this law? What problem did this law address?** These questions cannot be correctly answered without an understanding of ancient Near Eastern cultures. Recall that one of the primary reasons something is mentioned in the Pentateuch is to highlight beliefs and practices where the Israelites were to be different than the surrounding cultures.

In ancient Near Eastern cultures, if a man dismissed or abandoned his wife, he could reclaim her several years later though she had married another man and had children with her second husband[23]. Not only was her first husband able to reclaim her, but he could also claim, as his own, any children from her second "marriage." In agrarian societies, children are a valued asset. This could be a significant financial motive for the first husband to take her back. Thus, a primary reason for the bill of divorce mentioned in Deuteronomy 24:1-4 was to protect divorcées, giving them the legitimate and legal right to marry again and to remain married without fear of their first husbands reclaiming them. This legal document severed the marital bond and freed the divorcée to remarry without civil or religious sanctions. "It provided a clean and proper end to a broken marriage."[24]

There is also significant evidence indicating that Deuteronomy 24:1-4 mentions **two different kinds of divorce**. Notice the contrast between the first and second divorce. The first divorce, mentioned in verse one, was because the wife found no favor in her husband's eyes, because he "found some matter of uncleanness in her." "Uncleanness" comes from the Hebraic word עֶרְוָה 'ervâh, *er-vaw'*, meaning nakedness, shamefulness, blemish or disgrace. This divorce would likely have ended in the woman losing all or part of her dowry because she had transgressed the marriage covenant in some manner. There was presumably a legitimate and morally acceptable reason for the husband to divorce his wife—a shameful or disgraceful act or lifestyle.

This "legitimate" reason could have been a refusal to fulfill her end of the marriage covenant (specified and understood obligations) in food preparation, bearing children, caring for their children, taking care of the household, refusal of the husband's conjugal rights, etc. This was understood in their culture and governed (to a limited degree) by their local civil governments. Extended family members would have also significantly influenced such decisions concerning divorce. It is highly unlikely that "uncleanness" referred to adultery or some other sexual sin, before or after they were married, because Moses dealt specifically with such cases in other passages.

The second divorce, mentioned in verse three, is due to the husband detesting or hating his wife. It was a "hateful" divorce, apparently due to the bad attitude and/or selfish motives of the husband and not the errant actions or detestable traits of the wife. This divorce would have ended with the wife retaining her dowry because there was no "legitimate" reason for the divorce. Similarly, the wife would have retained her dowry if she were widowed. In either case there could have been a significant financial motive for her first husband to desire to marry her again.

Moses, by the inspiration of God, established the law of divorce in order to protect women from being treated sadistically and to elevate women's rights allowing them to legally remarry and remain married! The law of divorce also kept women from being seduced back into relationships through which they had already suffered rejection.

King David's marriage to Michal, King Saul's daughter, is a biblical example of a man reclaiming his wife after having abandoned her and she having married another man. David married Michal after paying the gruesome bride price demanded by King Saul of killing one hundred Philistines (I Samuel 18:20-28). Requiring the death of one hundred Philistines was one of the initial indirect attempts of King Saul to have David killed. King Saul's jealousy and hatred of David continued to grow until Saul set aside all pretence and openly conspired to kill him.

Michal helped David escape; but in the course of events, he abandoned her, leaving her to suffer the wrath of her deranged father, King Saul (I Samuel 19:9-17). Over the next ten to fifteen years, Saul made several attempts at trapping David, but they all failed. During this time David married Ahinoam and Abigail; and Saul arranged for Michal to marry another man, Palti (I Samuel 25:43-44).

King Saul eventually died along with Jonathan, his firstborn son. Another son of Saul, Ishbosheth, was made King of Israel, but civil war erupted and the tribe of Judah broke away from the union and made David their king. Following this, Israel consistently lost battles against Judah for seven and a half years. Toward the end of this period of time, Abner, Ishbosheth's top general, conspired with David to reunite Israel and make David king over all. During their deliberations, David demanded that Michal be given back to him as a prerequisite for him taking the throne of Israel.

The Bible does not state David's motive for this demand. From the way the incident is recorded, though, it sounds like it was primarily a political move for David, positioning himself to be King of Israel. Michal was King Saul's daughter, a princess of Israel. Thus, from a political perspective, her husband would be a rightful heir of the throne. One must also take into consideration that David was separated from Michal for ten to fifteen years or even longer, and she was "married" to Palti for almost that entire time. During that time, it is not recorded that David ever attempted to regain her as his wife, either by force, abduction, or negotiation, either before Saul's death or after.

On the other hand, Palti's love for Michal is evident as revealed in that he shamelessly wept as he followed along behind the caravan that took her away. *"So Ishbosheth took Michal away from her husband Palti son of Laish. Palti followed along behind her as far as Bahurim, weeping as he went. Then Abner told him, "Go back home!" So Palti returned"* (II Samuel 3:15-16 NLT). Apparently, Palti loved Michal passionately. He followed her all the way to the border of Judah, where Abner, the captain of the armies of Israel, commanded him to go back home. To go any further could have caused problems in the exchange and been embarrassing for Ishbosheth and Abner.

What a tragic story! Michal loved David enough to suffer the wrath of her father, King Saul; and yet it is not recorded that David ever attempted to get her back before or after she was given to another man. Apparently, David's primary and possibly only motivation for reclaiming her as his wife was political—to help establish him in the opinions of others as the rightful heir of the throne of Israel. By then Michal had been married to Palti for ten to fifteen years, and it is obvious that he loved her dearly; but David had her forcibly taken away from him. David did this, though he had already married two other women. It is probable that Michal never fully embraced David again and even came to despise him. Sadly, she remained childless for the remainder of her life (II Samuel 6:16-23), a tragic ending for a Princess and Queen of Israel. If a Princess of Israel, God's people, was treated this way, one can only imagine the horrors that the common woman faced in the ancient Near East!

The tragedy of Michal's life is compounded even today by her reputation being tarnished, marred by ministers that use her as a negative example of who not to be like. I have often heard ministers say something like, "Don't be like Michal, who despised David worshipping God. If you do, God will cause you to be barren also!" What a terrible thing to say! It is true that we should not despise people worshipping differently or with more passion and exuberance than we do. If we despise others who worship differently than ourselves, we could experience barrenness, a *leanness of soul,* that is the result of having such a prideful attitude. But Michal is not an example of this! This accusation of Michal comes from an errant interpretation of the final scene in the biblical account of her life.

After taking Michal from Palti and being crowned King of Israel, David decided to move the Ark of the Covenant to Jerusalem. During the procession, David worshipped the Lord with passionate abandonment. In doing so, he stripped to where he only wore a linen cloth. This upset Michal tremendously, who said,

> *You acted like a dirty old man, dancing around half-naked in*
> *front of your servants' slave girls. David told her, 'The Lord*
> *didn't choose your father or anyone else in your family to*
> *be the leader of his people. The Lord chose me, and I was*
> *celebrating in honor of him. I'll show you just how great I*
> *can be! I'll even be disgusting to myself. But those slave-girls*
> *you talked about will still honor me!' Michal never had any*
> *children* (II Samuel 6:20-23 CEV). (emphasis mine)

Michal was not upset with David for worshipping the Lord radically or otherwise. She was upset with him (as she perceived it) for strutting his stuff in front of other women; and more than likely she was still bitter towards him for abandoning her and then wrecking her second "marriage," having her forcibly taken from a man that dearly loved her. We must also remember that David had a tremendous lust for women as evidenced by him eventually having over three hundred wives, and bringing much destruction upon all of Israel for his adultery with Bathsheba. It is therefore possible that Michal's judgment of David was based on truth, to a greater or lesser degree, indicating that David had mixed motives in his actions while worshipping before the Lord. This is probable; who among us are totally pure in our worship and service of God, or for that matter, in any aspect of our lives? The best we have to offer is completely polluted with our selfish nature!

After this spat between husband and wife, it is then noted, sadly so, that Michal never had any children. This could have simply been due to a physical problem. This is probable considering that she did not have any children during her initial marriage to David when in Saul's house, during her "illegal and illegitimate marriage" to Palti, or during her reunion with David after he had her taken from Palti. It is also possible that she and David were never again intimate after their heated argument; David certainly had plenty of other wives to choose from to fulfill his personal needs and desires.

Her barrenness could have also been due to her father, Saul's sin against God. Due to his disobedience, God rejected Saul as King of Israel (I Samuel 15), and declared that the kingdom would be given to another man, and thus his dynasty would not continue. This "curse" could have spiritually affected Michal, causing her to be barren and thus not leaving an heir that might continue the line of Saul. Frankly, I believe that this is the probable source of Michal's barrenness. The significant thing to note, however, is that the Bible in no way indicates that Michal was barren because of despising David worshipping God!

Although tragic, Michal's story does provide an important example of the reason for Moses' legislation of the bill of divorce. The motivation behind the bill of divorce was compassion. It empowered an abandoned or expelled wife to remarry and remain married without fear of her first husband reclaiming her years later. The bill of divorce was meant to correct this sadistic ancient Near Eastern cultural practice.

When David abandoned Michal, he did **not** give her a bill of divorce. Therefore, Michal's marriage to Palti, although arranged and sanctioned by her father, King Saul, was not a marriage at all, according to civil law, but was an illegal adulterous relationship! It was an illegitimate, illegal marriage. David thus caused Michal to commit adultery by abandoning her; and the man that married Michal, Palti, committed adultery by marrying her. This sounds like something Jesus said, *"whoso marrieth her which is put away doth commit adultery"* (Matthew 19:9 KJV); and *"whosoever shall put away his wife, ... causeth her to commit adultery"* (Matthew 5:32 KJV). We will look at these passages in-depth later in the book.

The bill of divorce was unique to Israel in biblical times. There is no record of any other ancient Near Eastern culture making provision for such a document. The closest thing to it is an Assyrian bill of widowhood that was provided for a woman whose husband had been taken away as a captive by another nation. After two years, the woman could assume that her husband was dead and ask for a bill to be drawn up that would allow her to legally marry another man.

To "put away" a wife was to abandon, desert, or expel her from the household. A woman who was put away without a bill of divorce was relegated, at best—to a life of abject poverty, at worst—to a life of adultery and even prostitution. To "put away" a wife without a bill of divorce was cruel, hard-hearted, treacherous, and sadistic.

To "put away" comes from the Hebraic word גָּרַשׁ **gârash** *gaw-rash* , meaning to put away, expel, or thrust out. Whereas "divorce" comes from the Hebraic word כְּרִיתוּת, **kᵉrîythûwth,** *ker-ee-thooth,* meaning divorce, a cutting of the matrimonial bond. Although **gârash** is closely related to **kᵉrîythûwth** and is translated as "divorce" in many modern translations, it is important to distinguish between these two words so that we can better understand Jesus' comments concerning this passage.

Sadly, though the bill of divorce was meant to bring increased freedom into the lives of abandoned women by empowering them to legally remarry and to remain married, it became a means of stopping some women from divorcing their husbands, even though their husbands broke understood stipulations of their marriage covenants. Deuteronomy 24:1-4 came to be interpreted in Israel to mean that the husband must be the one to write the bill of divorce or at least sign it; the wife could not. Therefore divorce became the prerogative of the husband.

Furthermore, no legal provisions were made for wives whose husbands came up missing due to war or tragedy while traveling, much less for those whose husbands deliberately abandoned them. These women could not legally marry another man no matter how long their husbands were missing. Orthodox Jewish communities struggle with this issue to this day; although some Jewish women obtain civil divorces, Orthodox Rabbinical leadership does not recognize these divorces as valid. This is what happens when law becomes isolated from the spirit behind and purpose for which it was written!

On the other hand, requiring a certificate of divorce to be written strengthened marriages and added weight to the decision to break a marriage covenant. Divorce was not something that should be done in the heat of the moment; rather, it was something that took time, required the witness of others, and sometimes the intervention of judges, thus increasing civil oversight to aid in the protection of women.

Another benefit of the divorce certificate was the establishment of a specific point in time for the settlement of the financial aspect of the divorce– the dowry. If it was a "hateful" divorce, one based on selfish illegitimate reasons on the husband's part, the wife would be given the entire dowry. If the husband could provide ample evidence of a legitimate reason to divorce his wife, the judges might only require him to pay a fraction of the dowry, if any. But whether the divorce was based on legitimate or illegitimate reasons, it was legal, valid, and final. In either case, the wife was free to marry another man. This was a specific part of the wording in the certificate of divorce; and of course considering that polygamy was legal, the husband was free to marry at any time, unless otherwise specified in a current marriage covenant by which he was bound.

As mentioned earlier, Moses was clear and specific regarding marital laws. In Deuteronomy 24:1-4, however, he was non-specific, even vague. Moses made a generalized statement recognizing that men divorce their wives for a variety of reasons—legitimate and illegitimate. Moses clearly did not provide specific civil legislation concerning acceptable reasons for divorce. Why?

The following is reasonable speculation and nothing more; I believe that Moses understood that civil legislation could not adequately address the conundrum of establishing acceptable or non-acceptable reasons for divorce. Divorce is the result of a problem of the heart that is impossible to regulate via civil law. If a husband or wife has a hardened heart against his or her spouse, the marriage covenant will be broken in some way. In fact, today "It is commonly accepted among sociologists that there is no necessary relationship between the actual reasons for which a couple seeks divorce and the legal grounds they use in the divorce suit."[25] Only God can discern the motives of the heart. This will be discussed further when we look at Jesus' comments about Deuteronomy 24:1-4.

# Chapter IX
# THE "PLAIN" TEXT

KATHLEEN

Kathleen is a lovely young mother with a rambunctious fun-loving boy and one of sweetest little girls ever created by God. Kathleen loves Jesus with a passion because He has delivered her from a potentially lethal lifestyle and relationship. After coming to know the Lord, she found the personal courage and social support that she needed to divorce her abusive husband.

Due to her husband's abuse, Kathleen feared for her life and the lives of her children. Upon the counsel of a dear friend and pastor, Kathleen not only divorced her husband but also moved to the other side of the continental United States of America. God soon blessed her with a good job and has brought much healing into her and her children's lives. She's active in ministry and loved by all that know her. A nice young man fell in love with her and asked her to marry him.

"Now for the rest of the story," as Paul Harvey would say. Upon hearing of her engagement, the pastor that helped Kathleen through her divorce and relocation wrote her a hurtful email. He said that it grieved him very much to write it, but he felt that he must be true to his beliefs. In no uncertain terms, he told Kathleen that she did not have a "scriptural" divorce (her ex-husband had not committed adultery, although he was abusive); therefore she could not remarry, but must live celibate the remainder of her life. He believed that God would not recognize or honor, much less bless, her second marriage. Although what he wrote hurt Kathleen terribly, she was going to marry anyhow.

Sadly, due to other circumstances, the engagement was later broken off. Hearing of this, the pastor wrote another note expressing that he believed that God had found a way to keep her from making a terrible mistake. Kathleen questioned if her friend/pastor was right and began to lose hope that she could ever have a loving marital relationship and that her children could have a loving father.

Kathleen, the good news is that God loves you. He has set you free in heart and soul; and you are no longer bound to your ex-husband. You are free to remarry, as you will in the Lord. Continue to look to God for all your needs and He will provide wonderfully for you and your children. Do not let others bring you under false religious bondage! Whom the Son has set free, is free indeed! (John 8:36)

Matthew 5:31-32, 19:3-12, Mark 10:2-12, and Luke 16:18 comprise Jesus' comments about marriage and divorce. They are used as the primary scriptural support for the traditional doctrine of divorce and remarriage. However, there is abundant evidence to support a completely different interpretation than what is commonly believed in Christendom!

We will examine closely each "difficult" passage. They are commonly referred to as "difficult," because they seem to be unusually harsh, even unjust; and to most Christians, they do not sound like something that Jesus would say. Furthermore, if one accepts them at face value, they are difficult to apply in the lives of an increasingly large percentage of the population, divorcées. Below, I have quoted modern translations because they dynamically convey the traditional interpretation of these difficult passages, especially the phrases underlined.

Matthew 5:31 & 32, (NLT)
*You have heard that the Law of Moses says, "A man can divorce his wife by merely giving her a letter of divorce." But I say that a man, who divorces his wife, unless she has been unfaithful, causes her to commit adultery. And anyone who marries a divorced woman commits adultery.*

Matthew 19:8 & 9 (NCV)
*Jesus answered, "Moses allowed you to divorce your wives because you refused to accept God's teaching, but divorce was not allowed in the beginning. I tell you that anyone who divorces his wife and marries another woman is guilty of adultery. The only reason for a man to divorce his wife is if his wife has sexual relations with another man".*

Mark 10:10-12 (NKJV)
*In the house His disciples also asked Him again about the same matter. So He said to them, "Whoever divorces his wife and marries another commits adultery against her. And if a woman divorces her husband and marries another, she commits adultery".*

Luke 16:18 (CEV)
*It is a terrible sin for a man to divorce his wife and marry another woman. It is also a terrible sin for a man to marry a divorced woman.*

Proponents of the traditional theology of marriage and divorce speak of the plain, clear, straightforward, and self-evident meaning of these passages. They call us to set aside personal misgivings, concerns, questions, experiences, and emotions that might disagree with the "plain" meaning of the text and embrace these passages as "clearly" interpreted, totally renouncing divorce and especially forbidding remarriage.

For most people, though, the "plain" meaning of these texts raises too many questions to blindly accept them at face value. How can they apply in today's culture of divorce? How does a divorcée commit adultery by marrying again; does God not recognize the divorce and still consider the divorcée married? Does God not recognize the second marriage? If so, is the couple living in sin, or, as some say, "living in adultery?"

Why is a divorced wife relegated to commit adultery when it is evident that the husband has sinned against her by not honoring their marriage covenant? To specifically punish the wife for the sins of the husband seems unjust and in no way fits the character of Christ, as most people know Him; how can this be?

Why does the Lord treat divorce with such unusual harshness? Did Jesus actually disagree with the Law of Moses concerning divorce? Why does this not follow the teaching pattern Jesus established throughout the remainder of the Gospels? Did Jesus intend to make the law of divorce much stricter, "giving teeth to the law" as some say?

Attempting to answer these questions, some scholars suggest that sexual intercourse with someone other than the original marriage partner is what breaks the marriage union, is this true? What about couples who remain married though one committed adultery? Was their marriage broken by the adultery, and then reestablished by their fornication though they were married? Others believe that these difficult passages are evidence that marriage is indissoluble and thus divorcées that have remarried are in adulterous relationships and not married in the "eyes of God." These are just some of the many questions and conjectures raised by these scriptures, as they are "plainly" interpreted, why?

Frankly, such confusion and complexity exists because these passages have been tragically misinterpreted for over eighteen hundred years, every since the Gentile, Greco-Roman church lost, ignored, and/or rejected most of Christianity's Jewish heritage. In doing so, these scriptures were isolated from their Jewish context (historical, cultural, and literary) and their original meaning was lost in an ocean of misinformation and false assumptions! The result is what is quoted above–harsh, condemning statements that in no way fit the Gospel or the character of Jesus Christ, the Messiah!

As a preface to examining these passages, it should be noted that there are several significant variations in the early Greek manuscripts of each of the more difficult texts. Matthew 5:32 has at least three different texts. One group of texts totally omits the part about a man committing adultery who marries a woman that has been divorced. Mark 10:12 has at least five different texts, and there are eight different texts of Matthew 19:9. Luke 16:18 has at least three variant texts in early manuscripts.

David Parker, Lecturer in New Testament at The University of Birmingham, author of *Codex Bezae: An Early Christian Manuscript and its Text*, and co-editor of *The International Greek New Testament Project,* wrote an astute article concerning the numerous variations in the Greek text of these difficult passages. He wrote the following:

Many church reports have struggled with the questions raised by these passages. On the whole, their examinations seem to have presupposed that each saying exists only in one text form. They could have advanced their studies considerably by looking at the bottom of the page and reading the *apparatus criticus*. They would have discovered that they were **grasping at shadows**. What we have is a collection of interpretative rewritings of a tradition. ... **the concept of a Gospel that is fixed in shape, authoritative, and final as a piece of literature, has to be abandoned. The invitation to pay heed to the words of Jesus is then freed from the demand to accept the authority of the text.** And the freedom with which the early churches altered the tradition to make sense of their own difficulties and conflicts is another invitation—**to find the living word of Jesus that spoke to the tradition and that continues to speak.**[26] (emphasis mine)

Please note that when Dr. Parker writes "Gospel," from the context of this quote, it is evident that he references ONLY the controversial verses, the difficult passages previously noted. In no way is he calling into question the authority of the entire word of God, especially the Gospels as a whole; but he does question our ability to distill an authoritative text for the verses under consideration–the difficult quotes of Jesus concerning divorce.

Why include this quote? **First**, due to the numerous variations in the early Greek manuscripts, we certainly must not rely completely or even heavily on these passages as a foundation for doctrine, especially any radical changes from the prevailing understanding of marriage, divorce, and remarriage as established in the remainder of the Bible! **Second**, in order to interpret these passages and arrive at an authoritative and redemptive message applicable for all generations and any situation—the "living word of Jesus"—due to their unstable nature we are even more so dependent than normal upon their context (cultural, literary, and authorial).

A statement worth repeating—a "Text" without a "Context" is a "Pretext." The "plain" meaning of these scriptures is not what Jesus meant at all! In fact, these texts have been so removed from their context, that they have become a pretext—an assumed interpretation that has hidden Jesus' true intention. We have already established the primary historical context when we reviewed the Mosaic Law. In the next few chapters, we will examine closely their cultural, literary, and authorial context, along with a few textual peculiarities. In the following chapter, we will examine an important element of the cultural context, the Pharisees.

# Chapter X
# SWALLOWING CAMELS

HYPOCRISY

*"Your pride has cut you off from the Body of Christ!"* This convicting statement echoed truth in my soul, laying bare the hidden motives of my heart!

Several months before receiving this chastisement from the Holy Spirit, I had received Christ as my Savior (been born-again) and was baptized in the Holy Spirit. Speaking in tongues and entering a new dimension of praise and worship were the primary evidences of this. The event of my salvation and being filled with the Holy Spirit radically changed my life. I was overwhelmed with a sense of awe at a new spiritual reality that opened up before me. I began studying the Bible and praying with a passion that I had never experienced or even dreamed existed. I also had a new and dynamic boldness in declaring His Word and sharing my faith.

One day as I was prayerfully studying the Bible, I read the story in Luke 7:36-50 of the woman who washed Jesus' feet with her tears. I had read this story hundreds of times before, yet that day was different. You might remember the story. Simon, a Pharisee, invited Jesus to his house for a meal. Jesus gladly went home with Simon; but, in the middle of the meal, a woman with a bad reputation came in, knelt behind Jesus, and began uncontrollably weeping. She cried so much that Jesus' feet became wet with her tears. Then she did the unthinkable; she touched Jesus in public. She actually began washing his feet with her tears. Then, dare I repeat it; she let her hair down and began drying His feet with her hair. Adding further insult, she took an expensive box of fragrant ointment and poured it on his feet. What a waste! What an insult! This woman was as bold as Jezebel was!

Simon the Pharisee was incensed; how could this woman dare to do something so … so … so unthinkable? In his home, furthermore! More than that, if Jesus was a true prophet, surely He would know what kind of woman this was. He would rebuke her; and as punishment for her sins, He would most certainly chastise her publicly and reject her from his presence! How could a "prophet" let himself be so publicly defiled by allowing such a woman to touch him? A true prophet of God would never act so shamefully!

Jesus, however, judged people by their hearts and not by their outward appearance, social status, or even their sinful lifestyles. He taught that all people were valuable and worthy of love and respect because they are objects of God's affection, the beat of His heart! In response to Simon's negative thoughts, Jesus tells the parable of two debtors. One man owed ten times as much as the other man; but neither could repay their debt. The moneylender magnanimously forgave both debts. Jesus then asked Simon which man would love and appreciate their benefactor the most. Stewing in self-righteous indignation over this woman's actions and Jesus' apparent appreciation of her, Simon is baffled as to why Jesus tells this story and yet smugly answers that the man who had been forgiven the most would love the benefactor the most. Jesus then said,

Luke 7:43b-47 (NKJV)
*"You have rightly judged." Then He turned to the woman and said to Simon, "Do you see this woman? I entered your house; you gave Me no water for My feet, but she has washed My feet with her tears and wiped them with the hair of her head. "You gave Me no kiss, but this woman has not ceased to kiss My feet since the time I came in. "You did not anoint My head with oil, but this woman has anointed My feet with fragrant oil. "Therefore I say to you, her sins, which are many, are forgiven, for she loved much. But to whom little is forgiven, the same loves little."*

As I read this passage, verse forty-seven impacted me differently than ever before. *"Therefore, I tell you, her many sins have been forgiven–for she loved much. But he who has been forgiven little loves little"* (Luke 7:47). I recall saying, "Jesus, I love you. You know that I love you; and yet, I've led a pretty moral life. I haven't fallen into the kind of sinful lifestyle that this woman had. I don't think that I should go and sin more so that I can love you more. So what can I do? I want to love you with all of my heart and passion. What can I do to love you more?"

Have you ever noticed that God often doesn't give you what you ask for, but always gives you what you really need? In this case, I did not even know what to ask for? I realize now, that there was nothing that "I could do" to love God more, but *God* could do something, and did, and is!

A few months later, having forgotten about this prayer, I was praying about other concerns. I don't remember what I was praying about, but I remember the encounter with Jesus. As I was praying, I received a vision. I saw a right hand lying on the ground. It had been cut off from its body. It was as if I was looking through the eyes of the body that had lost the hand. To my right side, there was a clear tube coming from mid-air. Its source I did not see. Blood flowed through the tube, into the hand, and out onto the ground, keeping the hand alive but making a bloody, muddy mess. The hand was still twitching. It was a horrific sight!

I then heard the Lord say; *"Your pride has cut you off from the body of Christ."* The motives of my heart were revealed and I understood that my pride predisposed me to refuse to receive the Spirit and Word of God through any other member of the body of Christ. I had come to a place of such spiritual pride, that I would not receive instruction, much less correction from other believers. I thought that I had a direct line to God and did not need others to speak into my life. My pride had also disabled me from being a blessing to others. In fact, my prideful attitude was causing the body of Christ tremendous pain. Although I still felt the Spirit of God (the blood) flowing in and through my life, I was spiritually sick and dysfunctional and would eventually die if not reconnected to the body.

Sometimes, the truth hurts. This time, it most certainly did! I was pierced to the heart, repenting in tears and crying out for God's forgiveness. I then saw the left hand pick up the right hand and reattach it to the right wrist. As the left hand passed over the wound, it was totally healed. In fact, there was no scar or evidence that the right hand had ever been cut off. I had been restored to the body of Christ, but my pride and self-righteousness had only begun to be dealt with!

Shortly after this experience, I was again prayerfully reading the Bible, reviewing Mathew 23 where Jesus castigates the religious leaders of His day, calling them hypocrites, snakes, a den of vipers, and sons of hell. As I came to the close of this section of scripture, the Lord spoke clearly to me saying, *"That's the way you are."* There was no anger or disgust in His voice, only the love of a father sternly and yet compassionately chastening his son.

Again, I was cut to the heart with truth. I realized that much of what I did was motivated out of selfish ambition and a desire to look good in the eyes of others. It was as if God had opened my heart, revealing the vile and putrefied poison that filled it. Oh how I cried! I cried for two weeks. To this day I cry when I think of it. The ugliness in my own soul was/is too much for me to handle. Except for the comfort of the Holy Spirit and the assurance of His forgiveness, I would have gone stark raving mad.

My prayer was answered. I had been forgiven much—much more than mere adultery or murder. I have been forgiven of my pride and self-righteousness, the most hideous and deceptive of all sin. When you think about it, the only people who are recorded as ever eliciting an angry response from Jesus were hypocrites, of whom I was one.

To this day, Jesus continues to answer my prayer to love Him more. He does this primarily through uncovering my wickedness and enabling me to repent and receive His abundant forgiveness. *"Therefore, I tell you, her many sins have been forgiven-for she loved much. But he who has been forgiven little loves little"* (Luke 7:47). May we all wash His feet with our tears of repentance and gratitude! You see, it's not how much we've sinned that's important, but how much of His forgiveness that we've received, and how much repentance has come to our lives.

In the parable of the two debtors, it really doesn't matter that one owed ten times as much as the other. One debt may have been a million times greater than the other was. What is important is that both recognized that they owed far more than they could ever repay. The penalty for both was the same— imprisonment for them and their families for the rest of their lives. They were both 100% forgiven and should have been equally grateful! In like manner, we are all impoverished sinners before the Lord of Creation and can only stand in amazement at His wonderful grace and forgiveness.

## THE PHARISEES

I have shared this personal story as an inspirational introduction to a potentially dry, but necessary, section about the Pharisees. It contains a significant amount of historical information; but hang in there. Understanding who the Pharisees were, their predominant philosophies and attitudes, and what they taught, is a vital key to unlocking the mystery of Jesus' difficult comments concerning divorce. Of course, people who enjoy history will find this chapter fascinating!

The political and social environment of Israel at the time of Christ was charged with unrest and dissention. The Pharisees were a Jewish sect, the largest, and held significant political and religious influence in Israel at the time of Christ, ruling as civil judges through the Sanhedrin, the Jewish Supreme Court, and as rabbis, being respected religious teachers. Another much smaller sect, the Sadducees, controlled the priesthood, holding the highest positions. The Sadducees were secular in their approach to religion and life, were favored by the Romans, and considered themselves the aristocracy of Israel. They did not believe in the eternal nature of man's soul, rejected the belief in the resurrection from the dead, and denied the existence of angles or spirits. The Sadducees also rejected the Oral Law as inspired or authoritative, only accepting the Written Law as obligatory. They quickly disappeared from history shortly after the destruction of the Temple, the loss of the priesthood, and any semblance of aristocracy in Israel. Their secular approach to life could not hold up under persecution.

Unlike the Sadducees, the Pharisees believed in the eternal nature of man's soul, the resurrection from the dead, angles, evil spirits, and held the Oral Law as obligatory. They believed that the Oral Law was passed down from Moses from one generation of rabbis (sages) to the next by word of mouth. The Oral Law was also known as the Traditions of the Elders.

The Pharisees believed that the Oral Law held as much, if not greater, authority than the Written Law held. If there was a contradiction between the Oral Law and the Written Law, the Oral Law was believed to be more accurate because it was the explanation of the Written Law. It was then and is even taught today in Jewish communities that one cannot understand the Written Law, without the Oral Law. Concerning influence and longevity, the Jewish religion of today, by in large, traces its descent through the centuries from the Pharisees.

This Oral Law was not recorded until after the destruction of Jerusalem (AD 70) and the failure of the Bar Kachba Rebellion (AD 132-135). After squashing the Bar Kachba Rebellion, the Roman Emperor Hadrian instituted a plan to erase the Jews from the land of Israel. He leveled Jerusalem to the ground and built another city on top, which he named Aelia Capitolina and forbade the few Jews who remained in the area from entering the city. The only day that Jews were allowed to enter the city was the 9th of Av, so that they could be reminded of their greatest defeat—the complete destruction of the Temple. The only parts that remained of the temple were some of the retaining walls surrounding the Temple Mount. The *Kotel*, a section of the Western Wall that was dubbed the "Wailing Wall," was the only piece of those retaining walls that the Jews could access for hundreds of years. This is where Jews came to weep and pray.

To further demoralize the Jews, Hadrian renamed Israel calling it *Philistia* (Palestine) after the Philistines who were ancient, bitter enemies of the Jewish people. This name survived through the centuries and was resurrected in 1917, after WWI, when the British took over the Middle East, having conquered the Ottoman Empire. They named the lands east and west of the Jordan River, the Palestine Mandate, including the country of Jordan, which the British created in 1923.

Hadrian also purposefully focused oppression on Jewish rabbis in order to expunge the monotheistic Jewish religion, forcing the Jews to assimilate further the pagan polytheistic Greco-Roman culture. It was during this time of tremendous oppression of the Jewish people, that rabbis began discussing what was previously unthinkable—recording the Oral Law!

Following the rule of Hadrian arose a time of relative peace for the Jewish people. It was during this period that a wealthy and influential rabbi, Yehudah HaNasi (Judah, the Prince), managed to befriend the Roman emperors who succeeded Hadrian, particularly Marcus Aurelius. Rabbi Yehudah HaNasi is such an important figure in modern Jewish history that he is affectionately referred to in Jewish scholarship as only *Rebbe*.

The Pharisees believed that the Oral Law was given at Mount Sinai, along with the Written Law. The Oral Law was an explanation in the practical application and meaning of the Written Law. Supposedly, it was passed verbally from generation to generation, and was never written because it was meant to be fluid, adapting as the times and circumstances warranted. However, Rabbi Yehudah HaNasi foresaw that the Sanhedrin, the central legal institution of the Jewish people during the time of Christ, might cease to exist because of the oppression of the Roman Empire, like the priesthood did with the destruction of the Temple. Two centuries after the time of Rabbi Yehudah HaNasi, in the fourth century, the Sanhedrin did cease to exist.

To make sure the Oral Law was not lost altogether, from AD 170 to AD 200, Rabbi Yehudah went to many rabbis asking them to recite as much as they could remember of the Oral Law. He recorded the information and edited it, resulting in the Mishna.

The Mishna was completed in AD 219. Soon thereafter the rabbis in Israel and Babylon decided that more information needed to be recorded. The Mishna was written in a shorthand fashion with the assumption that the reader would be well acquainted with the subject material. Over the next few hundred years, rabbis in Israel and Babylon recorded their discussions concerning passages of the Mishna, resulting in the Babylonian and Jerusalem Talmuds.

Due to the ongoing Roman oppression of the Rabbis in Israel, the Jerusalem Talmud is much shorter and not as well edited, making it more

124 GOD IS A DIVORCÉ TOO!

difficult to understand. Things being much more stable in Babylon afforded the rabbis in that province ample opportunity for extended discussions concerning each passage in the Mishna. This resulted in the Babylonian Talmud, a veritable encyclopedia of Pharisaical thought during and after the time of Christ! Today, Jewish rabbinical students study the Babylonian Talmud as a primary source of religious inspiration and authority. The Jerusalem Talmud is not usually taught, even in the most Orthodox Jewish schools, though advanced scholars sometimes study it. Generally when someone cites the Talmud, they reference the Babylonian Talmud, as I do in this book henceforth.

Is it possible that the Pharisaical concepts, philosophies, and teachings that were prevalent in the time of Christ are recorded and available today? Yes! The teachings of the Pharisees are available to us in the Babylonian Talmud and can help us understand the cultural context of what Jesus said and did. How did Jesus feel about the Pharisees and their oral tradition? What did Jesus think of their teachings? In Matthew 23, He says:

*They make strict rules and try to force people to obey them, but they are unwilling to help those who struggle under the weight of their rules (v. 4). You are hypocrites! You close the door for people to enter the kingdom of heaven. You yourselves don't enter, and you stop others who are trying to enter (v. 13-14 NCV).*

*Woe to you, scribes and Pharisees, hypocrites! For you travel land and sea to win one proselyte, and when he is won, you make **him twice as much a son of hell as yourselves** (v. 15 NKJV).*

*Hypocrites! You are like whitewashed tombs—beautiful on the outside but filled on the inside with dead people's bones and all sorts of impurity. **You try to look like upright people outwardly, but inside your hearts are filled with hypocrisy and lawlessness** (v. 27-28). **Snakes! Sons of vipers! How will you escape the judgement of hell?** (v. 33 NLT) (emphasis mine)*

Can you hear the anger in His voice? Can you feel the absolute disgust that Jesus had for the teachings of the Pharisees? Filled with righteous indignation, Jesus forcefully denounces their twisted, perverted ideology and life-styles! Why?

I have often read or heard that Jesus opposed the Pharisees because of their legalistic, judgmental, controlling, condemning, prideful, and self-righteous attitudes. This was bad enough, but I had no idea concerning the depths of depravity that were condoned by their teachings. Truly, the Pharisees strained out gnats (legalism), and yet they also swallowed camels (license and lawlessness)!

## LEGALISM

Legalism is a common "religious," but ungodly approach to life. It is believed that life should be directed and controlled by external obedience to established laws, rather than through a personal internal motivation by the Spirit of God. Law is to rule every aspect of life, personal, domestic, religious, civil, and social. Law is often meant to conform people to the image of those in leadership, those making and enforcing the law. Law, and obedience to it, is believed to be the answer to the problems in life and society. Obedience to specified rules of conduct and life-style are believed to be the primary means of pleasing God and especially pleasing those who are in authority. These rules of conduct are not only a means of controlling one's personal life, but they are also a means of manipulating, controlling, and judging other people—primary goals of hypocritical, religiously minded people. The Beacon Dictionary of Theology defines legalism as:

> (1) a dependence on law keeping as a means of salvation, and/ or (2) an excessive bondage to the letter of the law which misses its intent and which fails to be motivated by love. ... The threat of legalism has plagued the church from the first century to the present. Today the appeal is not to adopt the Jewish law, but to drift into moralism, a "Christian" version of legalism. Law is viewed as the only alternative to a freedom that becomes license. Religion thus becomes primarily a matter of following a set of rules and regulations—works righteousness.[27]

The topic of law directing one's life as opposed to God directing one's life through a personal spiritual relationship is interesting. Law alone kills, but the Spirit of God gives life (II Corinthians 3:6). If we live by the Spirit though, we will fulfill the Law. The Law was given to teach us how to live and reveal our need of a savior, not to save us. Law is not the answer to life's problems. Law is not the answer to the plague of divorce either. The answer is in people having personal spiritual relationships with God! Through faith, we may be born of the Spirit of God, changed at the very core of our being, and have the Law of God written on our hearts. We are then motivated to walk in love for God and the love of God for our fellow man, especially those closest to us. Walking in this love perfectly fulfills the Law.

The Pharisees, however, excelled in legalism. The teachings of the Torah were divorced from their context and purpose, codified into a crushing burden, and used to condemn and oppress the ordinary person! The prime examples of this are the laws surrounding observance of the Sabbath. In the Talmud, a large section (24 chapters / 1806 pages) is devoted to Sabbath regulations. It is the second largest Tractate of the Talmud, being only exceeded by Baba Bathra, which deals with rights of ownership, regulating worldly affairs and business disputes.

One could justifiably conclude that Sabbath regulation was the Pharisees' sacred cow! The Sabbath Tractate starts off with things that may not be done on Friday, then discusses the oils and wicks which may be used in kindling the Sabbath lights; how food for the Sabbath should be stored, and then lists the principal labors which must be abstained from on the Sabbath. A complete chapter is devoted to circumcision on the Sabbath. Talk about straining out gnats! 1806 encyclopedic pages of regulations concerning the opening and closing of doors, what kitchen utensils may or may not be used, how many sins are committed when a person hands something through a door to another person standing outside, etc., creating a seemingly endless and pointless harangue of regulations, arguments, and debates!

Jesus purposefully did things to challenge such man-made rules and regulations. In Matthew 12 is recorded the story of Jesus and His disciples passing through a field and His disciples picking and eating some of the ripened grain. Of course, the Pharisees were watching and condemned them for doing so. Jesus corrects the Pharisees, pointing out that even David, when he was hungry, ate some of the bread dedicated to the priests which was unlawful for him to do, and even gave some to those with him.

Jesus calls their attention to the original purpose of the Law saying, *"The Sabbath was made to benefit people, and not people to benefit the Sabbath"* (Mark 2:27 NLT). Jesus further pressed the issue by going to the local synagogue and directly challenging the attitudes and teachings of the Pharisees. Seeing a man with a withered right hand, Jesus asked them if it was lawful to do good on the Sabbath or evil, to save life or to kill. But the Pharisees would not answer Him. Grieved by their callused hearts, Jesus commanded the man to stretch out his hand; and immediately it was healed, apparently regardless of whether or not the man had faith in Christ. Rather than rejoicing with the man, the Pharisees' response was to leave the synagogue and begin plotting with the Herodians, another political sect, how to destroy Jesus.

In another place, in Luke 13, Jesus healed a woman in a synagogue on the Sabbath. This was an "in-your-face" confrontation, purposefully challenging the teachings of the Pharisees. She had been bound with a spirit of infirmity for eighteen years. The ruler of the synagogue responded with indignation revealing the wickedness in his heart, saying that *"There are six days on which men ought to work; therefore come and be healed on them, and not on the Sabbath day"* (Luke 13:14 NKJV). Jesus then said to him,

> *"Hypocrite! Does not each one of you on the Sabbath loose his ox or donkey from the stall, and lead it away to water it? So ought not this woman, being a daughter of Abraham, whom Satan has bound—think of it—for eighteen years, be loosed from this bond on the Sabbath?"* *And when He said these things, all His adversaries were put to shame; and all the multitude rejoiced for all the glorious things that were done by Him* (Luke 13:15-17 NKJV).

On the Sabbath, Jesus also healed a blind man (John 9), a lame man by the pool of Bethesda (John 5), and a man whose arms and legs were swollen with dropsy (Luke 14). And these are only the ones recorded. There is no telling how many people he actually healed on the Sabbath! Each time was a purposeful challenge of the Pharisees' Oral Traditions concerning the Sabbath, the second largest Tractate in the Talmud! He was killing their sacred cow; it's no wonder that they responded with so much anger.

The spirit behind the Law of the Sabbath was meant to provide a day of rest from everyday work and to establish a pattern of worship in one's life and in the community. The Sabbath was meant to be a blessing, but legalism had made it a curse, making man serve the Sabbath!

Like arguing over the arrangement of deck-furniture on the Titanic, legalism makes a religious show of being important and authoritative concerning issues that have no importance, and yet all the while hiding failure in more important matters such as justice, mercy, and compassion!

LICENSE

The Pharisees were also given over to license and lawlessness. According to the Talmud, racism was not only condoned; it was commanded. Although plainly prohibited in the Written Law, in the Oral Law, Gentiles were considered non-human, compared to asses (Kethuboth 111a), and spoken of as barbarians. Considering Gentiles were non-human, they had no civil rights (Baba Kamma 37b). Gentiles were not considered "neighbors," thus any passages regarding neighbors did not apply to a Gentile.

It was against the law to teach a Gentile the Torah, punishable by death. *"A heathen who studies the Torah deserves death, for it is written, 'Moses commanded us a law for an inheritance,' it is our inheritance, not theirs"* (Sanhedrin 59a). If a Gentile studied the Law, he might use it to his advantage over a Jew, and the Pharisees certainly couldn't allow that. If a Jew found a lost article of a Gentile, it was permissible to keep it, thus legalizing theft (Baba Kamma 113b). Returning a lost article to a Gentile was even considered a sin (Sanhedrin 76b). Gentile property was considered unclaimed land (Baba Bathra 54b). Gentiles were not even allowed a day of rest (Sanhedrin 58b) though commanded in the Written Law (Exodus 20:10). Lawsuits between Jew and Gentile were always to result in favor of the Jew, regardless of guilt or innocence (Baba Kamma 113b). The essence of a long discussion in Sanhedrin 78b–79a is that not only is a Jew not liable if he kills a Gentile, but if a Jew accidentally kills another Jew while intending to kill a Gentile, he is not liable.

Not only was radical racism condoned and propagated, but so was every type of sexual perversion: adultery, fornication, sodomy, bestiality, incest, and even pedophilia (sexual perversion involving children). Though the Law of Moses clearly forbids such actions, the Pharisees interpreted the Written Law in such a way as to allow them to do whatever their wicked hearts desired. How could these things be condoned? A good example involves sodomy and pedophilia being condoned because the Bible says, *"Thou shalt not lie with mankind, as with womankind: it is abomination"* (Leviticus 18:22 KJV). The perverted Pharisaical mind argued that children are not *"mankind."* They do not become classified as "mankind" until a boy is nine or ten and girls are three (Sanhedrin 54b). Therefore, sodomy with children incurs no guilt for the adult. Those who commit pederasty with the dead are even exempt (Sanhedrin 78a). Is it any wonder that Jesus castigated them severely, calling them "sons of hell," and the Apostle Paul wished they would go ahead and castrate themselves!

Murder was legalized. A man was not held accountable for murder if he bound a man and the man subsequently died of starvation, dehydration, sunstroke, hypothermia, insect bites, or a lion. A man could kill his neighbor if he threw him into a pit and then removed the ladder before the man could climb out. Murder was legal if done with a bow and arrow, as long as a healing ointment was available, although immediately made unavailable to the dying man (Sanhedrin 77a). If a mob kills a man, no one is held accountable because no single person actually took the man's whole life. You may kill someone who has a fatal organic disease, a *terefah* (Sanhedrin 78a).

Swearing falsely was not only allowed, it was prepared for yearly by the Kol Nidre. *"And he who desires that none of his vows made during the year shall be valid, let him stand at the beginning of the year and declare, 'Every vow which I may make in the future shall be null. [His vows are then invalid,] providing that he remembers this at the time of the vow* (b.Nedarim 23a)." Vows were thus a means of deception, which was fully condoned by the Talmud. To think this type of activity is condoned and legislated in the Talmud, boggles the mind!

Of course, as is with any religious order, some adherents are more radical than others are in their interpretation and enforcing of the laws of their religion. This was the case with the Pharisees. Some were not as hard-hearted as others were, embracing the spirit of the law as opposed to trying to control others by the letter of the law. Nicodemus is possibly an example of this. He came to question Jesus at night, probably with a sincere heart seeking truth, hoping that they could talk without the distraction of crowds or other Pharisees trying to keep him or anyone else from really listening. Jesus did not reject him, but spoke to him of salvation (John 3).

Though Nicodemus could be an example of a "good" Pharisee, Jesus spoke of them as a group as sons of hell, blind guides leading the blind, perverse, and evil, wicked men.

> *Hypocrites! For you are careful to tithe even the tiniest part of your income, but you ignore the important things of the law—justice, mercy, and faith. ... Blind guides! You strain your water so you won't accidentally swallow a gnat; then you swallow a camel! ... You are so careful to clean the outside of the cup and the dish, but inside you are filthy—full of greed and self-indulgence!"* (Matthew 23: 23 – 24 NLT)

Jesus understood the evil behind their hypocritical cloak of religion, vilifying the Pharisees and their traditions. They were whitewashed tombs full of dead men's bones. They would strain out gnats from the wine so as not to eat something unclean, and then turn right around and gorge themselves on raw Camel meat, the largest unclean animal around, giving themselves over to all manner of perversion, evil, and wickedness. They made the word of God invalid by their traditions. As judges they did not do justice but oppressed people at every turn.

A book could be written on the evil of the Pharisees; but what has been shared is sufficient to paint a picture of the ideological, moral, and spiritual war between Jesus and the Pharisees. It is in this cultural context that the Pharisees tauntingly asked Jesus about the "Any Matter" divorce.

# *Chapter XI*
# THE "ANY MATTER" DIVORCE

## SHAMMAI AND HILLEL

At the time of Christ there were two predominant rabbinical schools of thought concerning divorce legislation. They both accepted the viability of divorce and numerous legitimate and morally acceptable reasons for divorce, but they differed significantly concerning divorce philosophy and procedures based on their respective interpretations of Deuteronomy 24:1.

When the High Priest Shimon HaTzaddik, the last leader of the Great Assembly brought together by Ezra, died in 273 BC, a period known as the "*Zugot,*" meaning "Pairs," began. From then, until the destruction of Jerusalem, there were always two rabbis that directed the work of the Sanhedrin. One was called the *Av Beit Din* (the head of the Sanhedrin), and the other was called the *Nasi* (the president). The last of the *Zugot* is probably the most famous— Shammai and Hillel.

Shammai (50 BC to AD 30) has a reputation, of being stern, stringent, and legalistic. His counterpart, "Hillel the Babylonian" or "Hillel the Elder" was much more a man of the people, having a reputation among Jews of being a man of patience and humility. Due to Hillel's contributions to rabbinical Judaism, he is compared to Ezra who also came from Babylon and reestablished the rule of the Torah in the land of Israel. Hillel served as *Nasi*, the president of the Sanhedrin, from 30 BC to AD 10.

The schools of Shammai and Hillel are famous for their disputes in Jewish law. In the Talmud many stories are recorded that give us insight into the lives of key people. One such story is recorded of Shammai and Hillel speaking with a heathen thinking of becoming a Jew.

> On another occasion it happened that a certain heathen came before Shammai and said to him, "Make me a proselyte, on condition that you teach me the whole Torah while I stand on one foot." Thereupon he repulsed him with the builder's cubit which was in his hand. When he went before Hillel, he said to him, "What is hateful to you, do not to your neighbor. That is the whole Torah, while the rest is the commentary thereof; go and learn it" (b.Shabbath 31a).

Of course, Hillel's response, although expressed in the negative, is similar to the Golden Rule, *"Do for others as you would like them to do for you"* (Luke 6:31 NLT).

Another such dispute concerned telling a bride on her wedding day that she is beautiful, even if it is not true. The school of Shammai was stern, asserting that it is wrong to lie. The school of Hillel disagreed, saying that a bride is always beautiful on her wedding day (b.Ketubot 16b – 17a). The disciples of Hillel had a reputation of being gentle and humble, studying the opinions of others and in their dissertations even mentioning them before their own.

## FOR ANY CAUSE

Every culture has words, phrases, and gestures that have unique meanings to that culture. Outsiders may easily misunderstand or completely miss the significance of such phrases or gestures. The Deep South (a culturally specific phrase itself meaning the Southeastern United States of America) has many such expressions: *just like peas and carrots, eatin' my grits, potbelly, yonder, redneck, y'all,* etc. This is typical of every culture. Of course, culture is a much larger category than just words and phrases. Culture involves traditions, customs, lifestyles, common morality, values, family structure, domestic issues, civil government and legislation, religion, religious sects, industry, etc.

Concerning the topic of divorce, there is recorded in the Talmud a significant dispute between the schools of Shammai and Hillel. This debate is alluded to in Matthew 19:3, which says, *"Some Pharisees came to him, and to test him they asked, 'Is it lawful for a man to divorce his wife for **any cause**?'"* (NRSV) (emphasis mine) The *"plain"* interpretation of this passage would lead one to believe that the discussion was about the establishment of legitimate reasons for divorce. However, the phrase "any cause," or "any matter," was a culturally specific Hebraic phrase that referenced the debate between the Hillelites and the Shammaites concerning the civil legislation of the "**Any Matter**" divorce philosophy and procedure, and specifically, the interpretation of Deuteronomy 24:1. Thus, the question in Matthew 19:3 was not about the establishment of acceptable or non-acceptable reasons for divorce, but about the viability of the "Any Matter" divorce proceedings.

Matthew's sister passage, Mark 10:2 says, *"Some Pharisees came, and to test him they asked, 'Is it lawful for a man to divorce his wife?'"* (NRSV) The plain interpretation of this passage would lead one to believe that the discussion was about the viability of divorce—could a man lawfully divorce his wife? The problem with this interpretation is that it would have been senseless, even absurd to the people of that day. All Jews knew and accepted that divorce was viable, because it was endorsed and regulated by the Mosaic Law. It would be about as senseless as asking today if it is lawful to quit your job.

Why would Mark leave out the phrase "Any Matter?" It is commonly accepted among biblical scholars that Mark wrote to a *Roman* audience, who would have not known of or understood the debate in Israel concerning the "Any Matter" divorce. He could have purposefully left this aspect out in order not to confuse his Roman audience. As we will see, the passage in Mark 10 is significantly different from the passage in Matthew 19. This will be discussed in depth in the chapter entitled "A Teachable Moment."

Matthew 5:31-32 and Luke 16:18 do not give a story context; so one can assume that they also relate to the "Any Matter" divorce debate. Their literary context involving the Pharisees and their similarity in wording to Matthew 19:9 confirms this. It would have been an understood assumption by the first century Jewish reader.

David Instone-Brewer provides significant extra-biblical support indicating that leaving out commonly understood information like this was typical in Jewish rabbinical literature. The author assumes that the readers would at least have a basic knowledge of the subject at hand.[28]

As previously noted, Moses did not establish acceptable or non-acceptable reasons for divorce, nor did He decree a specific divorce philosophy or proceeding, except the husband giving a bill of divorce to the wife he is putting away (Deuteronomy 24:1). However, the Pharisees, acting as civil judges, attempted to enforce specific divorce philosophies and procedures.

The debate between the Shammaites and Hillelites concerning the "Any Matter" divorce is mentioned in the Talmud in the last section in the last chapter of the tractate Gittin, folio 90a and 90b. Tractate Gittin is 439 encyclopedic pages of debate and legislation concerning the procedures for writing and presenting the bill of divorce, the "*get*." It does not concern itself with the morality of divorce, or acceptable or non-acceptable reasons for divorce.

## MORALLY ACCEPTABLE REASONS FOR DIVORCE

Both the Shammaites and Hillelites recognized a wide range of morally acceptable grounds for divorce including material neglect, emotional (conjugal) neglect, infertility, and of course adultery or other sexual misconduct. Material, emotional, and conjugal neglect were derived from Exodus 21:10 & 11 which says that if a man takes a slave as a wife and yet marries another woman also, he shall not diminish the slave wife's *"food, her clothing, and her marriage rights. And if he does not do these three for her, then she shall go out free without paying money"* (NKJV). There was a prevailing consensus among rabbinical writings for generations that if a slave wife had such rights, surely a wife who was not a slave should be treated equally well.

Concerning material responsibilities, the husband was expected to provide the basic raw materials for food and clothing, and the wife was expected to prepare the food and make the clothing, but it was not limited to this. For example, a woman could not be forced to live in a lesser dwelling than the one she was raised in. There were also regulations as to how far a wife could be forced to move away from her family without her consent, and a woman that lived in Israel certainly could not be forced to move outside of Israel. The penalty for a breach of the marriage covenant of a material nature could be divorce with the loss of all or part of the dowry for the guilty party.

Consistent denial of conjugal rights was also an issue that was legislated. A refusal to fulfill one's conjugal duties was handled differently than material neglect; the offending party was penalized financially. If the wife consistently rejected her husband, the dowry was reduced; and if the husband refused to fulfill his duties, the dowry was increased. Even the length of acceptable time for a husband to forgo his husbandly duties was regulated based on his occupation.

> He who takes a vow not to have sexual relations with his wife: The School of Shammai says, For two weeks, and the School of Hillel says, For one week. Disciples go forth for Torah study without consent for 30 days. Workers go for one week. The sexual duty of which the Torah speaks [Exodus 21.10]: those without work, every day; workers, twice a week; ass drivers, once a week; camel drivers, once in thirty days; sailors, once in six months – the words of R. Eliezer (m.Ketubot 5.6).
> She who rebels against her husband [re sexual duty] they deduct from her marriage contract seven denars a week. R. Judah says Seven tropaics. How long does one continue to deduct? – until her entire marriage contract [is voided]. R. Yose says, He continues to deduct for an inheritance may come from some other source from which he will collect what is due him. And similarly the rule for the man who rebels against his wife [re sexual duty] – they add three denars a week to her marriage contract. R. Judah says, Three tropaics (m.Ketubot 5.7).

Emotional neglect was handled via financial penalty in order to motivate the delinquent party into compliance and avoid divorce. However, the financial penalty did not have a practical application until the divorce was finalized or one of the parties passed away, thus inferring that at some point, if emotional neglect continues, divorce will occur. In either case, divorce or death, the dowry, increased or diminished, was given to the wife. Emotional neglect would have also included cruelty or humiliation; case law is recorded that deals with these issues. Abusive spouses were ordered to stop being cruel or divorce their spouses with full payment of the dowry.

Infertility was also accepted as a legitimate reason for divorce. Couples who were infertile for ten or more years and yet desired to remain together suffered significant social pressure to divorce and marry others in the hopes of producing offspring. Procreation was commonly believed to be the primary reason for marriage. Jews were expected to marry and produce offspring; to not do so broke one of the 613 laws of the Torah, *"be fruitful and multiply and fill the earth"* (Genesis 1: 28 KJV). During the time of Christ, infertility was a valid and even expected reason for divorce, although considered regrettable. *"The Shammaites as well as the Hillelites believed that childbearing was the prime motive for marriage, and they would therefore be disposed to grant divorce in this situation. However, there was likely some reluctance to do so."*[29]

Concerning fidelity in marriage—wives were expected to be faithful to their husbands. However, unless specifically stated in the marriage contract, husbands were not under any legal or social obligation of fidelity. For a married man, sexual intercourse with a woman other than his wife did not constitute adultery. Legally, it was only possible for a man, though married, to commit adultery via sexual intercourse with another man's wife. Even then, the man was not considered to have sinned against his *wife*, but against the *husband* of the woman with whom he committed adultery, assuming that man was another Jew.

## SOME UNCLEANNESS

Both the Shammaites and the Hillelites based their divorce philosophy and procedures on the nonspecific wording in Deuteronomy 24:1. *"When a man takes a wife and marries her, and it happens that she finds no favor in his eyes because he has found **some uncleanness** in her, and he writes her a certificate of divorce, puts it in her hand, and sends her out of his house"* (NKJV).

The debate was based on differing interpretations

of an unusual phrase in Deuteronomy 24.1 – עֶרְוַת דָּבָר 'ervâh dâbâr. This could perhaps be translated as "matter of indecency", though it is strange that the word "indecency" is in the construct form rather than the word "matter". Reading the phrase literally produces "indecency of a matter", or perhaps "nakedness of a matter." There was also another difficulty, as far as the Rabbis were concerned, because the word דָּבָר dâbâr ('matter') is apparently superfluous.[30]

The word דָּבָר dâbâr, *daw-baw';* means "a matter" or "a thing". The word עֶרְוָה 'ervâh, *er-vaw';* means "disgrace, blemish, uncleanness, etc." As was previously noted, when we examined Deuteronomy 24:1, these two words were in no way the focus of the passage; rather, they were used as a generalized description of the many reasons for which a man might divorce his wife. It is also likely that the phrase "a matter of indecency" indicated a divorce for "legitimate, morally acceptable" reasons, as opposed to the "hateful" divorce mentioned in verse three which was a divorce for "non-legitimate, morally non-acceptable" reasons. However, both divorces legally ended the marriage and freed the woman to remarry. Considering that polygamy was acceptable, the husband could never have been considered under any constraint not to remarry.

The following passage is the foundation of the rabbinical discussion in the Talmud concerning the "Any Matter" divorce debate between the Shammaites and Hillelites.

Mishnah. Beth Shammai say: A man should not divorce his wife unless he has found her guilty of some unseemly conduct, as it says, because he hath found some unseemly thing in her. Beth Hillel, however, say [that he may divorce her] even if she has merely spoilt his food, since it says, because he hath found some unseemly thing in her. R. Akiba says, [he may divorce her] even if he finds another woman more beautiful than she is, as it says, it cometh to pass, if she find no favour in his eyes (m.Gittin 9.10).

A cursory reading of this suggests that the debate concerns acceptable or non-acceptable reasons for divorce, but it was actually about the "correct" interpretation of Deuteronomy 24:1. From this verse, the Hillelites developed what was called the "Any Matter" divorce[31]. The "Any Matter" divorce essentially removed divorce from civil or public scrutiny. A man could divorce his wife without shaming her or himself by needing to publicly establish grounds for divorce. Rabbi Akiba affirmed the "Any Matter," no-fault divorce legislation highlighting the phrase *"find no favor in his eyes"* (Deuteronomy 24:1), interpreting it to possibly mean that the husband *"finds another woman more beautiful than she."*

The Shammaites, disagreed with the "Any Matter," no-fault divorce and required that evidence of a breach of the marriage covenant be produced, which effectively increased their influence and control. They could then determine who received the dowry, or how much of it. The amount of the dowry was determined by the severity of the wife's breach of the marriage covenant. With an "Any Matter" divorce, the dowry was not an issue; the husband paid it in full.

A secondary disagreement concerned the complexity of the stages involved in actually divorcing one's wife. The Shammaites were less stringent than the Hillelites concerning the method of divorce. Once a valid divorce document was created, the divorce was in effect even if the man never gave it to his wife. If he decided to keep her and never gave her the bill of divorce, she was still considered a divorcée, though now remarried.

The Hillelites were stricter concerning the method of divorce. For the Hillelites, there were three stages to a divorce, and each stage was strictly regulated. In order for the divorce to be valid, a husband must (1) write the bill of divorce, (2) put it into his wife's hand or her agent's hand, and (3) send her away. The husband must also fulfill any stipulations of the divorce and settle the dowry. These must be complete before the divorce was considered valid. Due to the ease of obtaining a bill of divorce, these stages and regulations possibly helped to delay the divorce, facilitate a meeting of the estranged couple, and hopefully promote reconciliation.

The viability of the "Any Matter" divorce proceedings was a well-known debate in Israel during the time of Christ. Not only Jewish rabbis, but the average person understood the basic concepts of this debate. It is also significant to note that although the Shammaites disagreed with the "Any Matter" divorce philosophy and proceedings, they accepted the "Any Matter" divorce as legal and binding, or shall we say, "legal and loosing." Shammaite rabbis would even perform wedding ceremonies for people who had previously been divorced using the "Any Matter" divorce proceedings. By the second century the debate was virtually settled except for continuing theological arguments. People chose to use the "Any Matter" divorce proceedings.

The "Any Matter" divorce was also part of the story of the birth of Christ. When Joseph found out that Mary, the mother of Jesus, was pregnant, he determined to *"put her away quietly"* (Matthew 1:19). This was an idiomatic, culturally specific way of saying that he was going to divorce Mary via an "Any Matter" divorce. Joseph was said to be a "just" man for choosing to use the "Any Matter" divorce, rather than publicly humiliating Mary by producing evidence of her breach of the marriage covenant. The "Any Matter" divorce was considered to be kinder than a Shammaite divorce.

Joseph chose the "Any Matter" divorce though he would have lost the financial investment that he had already made in the marriage, the bride price, not to mention personally crucifying the selfish nature of seeking revenge. Sadly, many commentaries on this passage miss this entirely, writing that Joseph's justness was due to him being a man of stern principles, as if these stern principles were the motivation for the divorce. This implies that a righteous man who has stern principles would never marry a woman that was not a virgin, or remain married to an unfaithful wife. That is plainly not the case; Joseph was considered a just man because he was willing to unselfishly use the "Any Matter" divorce proceedings in order to protect Mary from further shame and reproach. He was willing to divorce her without publicly humiliating her by taking her before a panel of Shammaite judges. This is a compelling argument in support of today's no-fault divorce legislation.

Unfortunately the "Any Matter" debate was not known or understood outside of the Jewish community. Therefore, even in the first century, non-Jewish believers outside of Israel would have struggled with correctly interpreting verses that directly or indirectly involved the "Any Matter" divorce. By the second century, the early church was far removed from its

Jewish heritage making it almost impossible for the Gentile Church Fathers to correctly interpret the difficult passages of Jesus concerning divorce in Matthew and Luke. History thus affirms Mark's decision in excluding the "Any Matter" debate from his account.

The "Any Matter" divorce is a **primary** element of the cultural context of the verses where Jesus speaks of divorce in Matthew and Luke. In order to interpret correctly these passages, it is vital that one understands that the debate was not about the viability of divorce, or about legitimate or illegitimate reasons for divorce, but about the good or evil of the "Any Matter" divorce philosophy and proceedings.

The rabbinical debate concerning polygamy is another element of the cultural context of Matthew 19 and Mark 10. Polygamy was practiced in Judaism until approximately the eleventh century when it was prohibited, and it is still practiced in Arabic countries of the Middle East. In support of their beliefs, rabbis who endorsed polygamy pointed out the many examples in their history of polygamous marriages that were accepted and recognized by God: Father Abraham, Patriarch Jacob, King David, King Solomon, etc. They could also point to the specific Mosaic Laws that regulated polygamous marriages, thus assuming that polygamy was legitimate and would continue: Exodus 21:10, 22:16, Deuteronomy 21:15-17, and 22:28. Furthermore, nowhere does the Mosaic Law forbid polygamy.

Rabbis who supported monogamy referenced the creation story and the story of Noah as proof text that monogamy is God's plan for marriage. Genesis 2:24 says, *"Therefore shall a man leave his father and his mother, and shall cleave unto his wife: and they shall be one flesh"* (KJV). Notice that the word *"two"* is missing from the phrase *"and they shall be one flesh."* The Hebraic text does not have the word, *"two,"* although it can be assumed from the literary context. Other ancient versions (Syriac Peshitta, Septuagint, and the Samaritan Pentateuch) added the word, *"two."* Rabbis who supported monogamy often quoted this verse using the word *"two"* in order to emphasis their point that marriage should consist of a husband and a wife, not a husband and several wives. Theologians today use a similar method of emphasizing what they believe to be true, quoting versions that most clearly endorse their beliefs.

Concerning our discussion of Jesus' words about divorce, it is significant to note that Jesus quoted Genesis 2:24 using the word, *"two." "The two shall become one flesh"* (Matthew 19:5, Mark 10:8). This alludes to Jesus' endorsement of monogamy as an important element of the "divine ideal" of marriage. One could also assume this from Jesus quoting this scripture in its literary context in Matthew 19 and Mark 10. But understanding the cultural context of these statements insures that we do not misunderstand Jesus' endorsement of monogamy as an element of God's plan for marriage.

From the cultural context, therefore, we gain significant insight into the words of Jesus concerning divorce. The question that the Pharisees asked Jesus in Matthew 19 had to do with the civil legislation of divorce, specifically concerning the "Any Matter" divorce philosophy and proceedings. Jesus was not asked concerning the viability of divorce in general, or morally acceptable or non-acceptable reasons for divorce, although that is what proponents of the traditional doctrine of divorce incorrectly assume. In Matthew 19 and Mark 10, we also find culturally significant wording that reveals Jesus' endorsement of monogamy.

# Chapter XII
# THE WHO BEHIND THE WHAT

In arriving at a text's authorial intent, what the author meant, another important element of the context is the "Who" behind the "What"—*the Authorial Context*. For example, sayings of political or religious "celebrities" are often taken out of context and published across the nation in headline news. But anyone who personally knows the celebrities knows that they would never say such a thing, or mean it the way that it comes across apart from its context or verbal tone. Therefore, without even knowing the literary context of the statement, people who know the author can question and even reject the statement's "*plain*" meaning, based solely on their personal knowledge of the author. Of course, this is subject to one's relationship with and knowledge of the author.

Who is Jesus? How did He relate to the Mosaic Law? What kind of person is He? What was the purpose of His earthly ministry? Who were His enemies and how did He relate to them? How did He relate to the divorcée? These are just a few of the questions we should ask concerning Jesus; the answers to which could significantly help us understand His intended meaning of the difficult passages concerning divorce.

Most of the books and articles that I have read that modify slightly or outright reject the traditional doctrine of divorce rely heavily upon the revealed goodness, forgiveness, and mercy apparent in the person of Jesus (rightly so in my opinion). If Jesus is forgiving, kind, and merciful with confessed sinners, why would He treat divorcées differently? How could He condemn a divorced woman to a life of either celibacy or adultery, especially considering her husband's hateful treatment of her?

The "plain" interpretation of the difficult passages on divorce do not sound at all like something Jesus would say, to most people who know Him. But this is subjective, depending on ones personal relationship with Jesus, or lack thereof. So let us look at a couple of objective aspects of Jesus and His ministry that directly effect how we should interpret the difficult passages on divorce.

One such element is Jesus' relationship with the Mosaic Law. Many theologians that write concerning these difficult passages assume that Jesus considered the Law of Moses concerning divorce, weak and inept. They assume that Jesus desired to strengthen the Law by affirming the "indissoluble" nature of marriage and renouncing divorce all together, thus giving teeth to the Law, making it much more strict.

Did Jesus disagree with the Law of Moses concerning divorce? In a word, No! Throughout His ministry, Jesus fully endorsed the Mosaic Law. Jesus said:

> *Don't think that I have come to destroy the Law of Moses or the teaching of the prophets. I have not come to destroy them but to bring about what they said. I tell you the truth, nothing will disappear from the law until heaven and earth are gone. Not even the smallest letter or the smallest part of a letter will be lost until everything has happened. Whoever refuses to obey any command and teaches other people not to obey that command will be the least important in the kingdom of heaven. But whoever obeys the commands and teaches other people to obey them will be great in the kingdom of heaven.* (Matthew 5:17 – 19 NCV).

Immediately preceding the difficult passage in Luke 16:18 Jesus says in verse 17, *"It would be easier for heaven and earth to pass away than for the smallest part of a letter in the law to be changed" (NCV).* Does it sound like Jesus wished to change the teachings of Moses concerning divorce or any other subject? Not at all! Based on these scriptures, we can only infer that Jesus agreed with the Law of Moses concerning divorce, and did not wish to change it. But the traditional "plain" interpretations of Jesus' words assume that Jesus intended to repudiate (reject as invalid) the Law of Moses concerning divorce.

Jesus came to give us abundant life, to fulfill the Messianic prophecies, to establish a New Covenant based on His death and resurrection (being the ultimate sacrifice), and to clarify issues that had become clouded by hypocritical teachers. Jesus came to write the Law of God on our hearts by the Holy Spirit, thus giving us power over sin. The Law in itself is righteous and holy; the problem is not with the Law but with the wickedness of our hearts.

There is absolutely no scriptural precedence to suggest that Jesus intended to change the Law of Moses concerning divorce! If anything, Jesus opposed and relaxed the stringent rules and regulations of the Pharisees that were supposedly built upon the Law, but were actually only the regulations of men. Jesus did not oppose or contradict the Law in any way, but He did oppose the Pharisees and their teachings. Jesus said of them, *"They tie up heavy loads and put them on men's shoulders, but they themselves are not willing to lift a finger to move them"* (Matthew 23:4 NIV). Today, could the traditional doctrine of divorce fit the category of a "heavy load?"

If we are to make an assumption about the intent of a passage, it must be based on the authorial context as much as possible. The more solidly an interpretation is based on the authorial context, the stronger the likelihood that the interpretation is correct. Did Jesus intend to change the Mosaic Law concerning divorce? No, He did not! Jesus assumed the full inspiration of the Old Testament, especially the Pentateuch; Moses' writings. Based on His revealed character and pattern of ministry, Jesus would have simultaneously endorsed the Mosaic Law, challenged the bad attitudes and false teachings of the Pharisees, and revealed the Spirit of God behind the Law, bringing conviction to the hearts of all present.

Another assumption that is important for us to note is our belief concerning Jesus' role in and relationship with civil government. Moses was instrumental in establishing civil and religious law and authority structures for the nation of Israel, serving as a religious prophet and a civil legislator. On the other hand, Jesus spoke as a prophet and not as a civil legislator.

Recall the story of the man who asked Jesus to tell the man's brother to divide the inheritance with him (Luke 12:13-15). Jesus responded, *"Man, who made me a Judge or an arbitrator over you? ... Take heed and beware of covetousness, for one's life does not consist in the abundance of the things he possesses."*

Jesus did not come to enforce, much less *develop* or *correct* civil law. Jesus came to call people to a new life in God. This new life would produce godly character and thus eradicate sin in our lives and empower us to live as godly citizens of any country, under any civil legislation. Jesus taught spiritual principles that dealt with root issues of sin in our hearts. He came to write the Law of God on our hearts, changing us at the core of our being. Jesus spoke prophetically concerning lawful living, but did not come to change the Mosaic Law, especially any civil law developed thereupon.

Understanding and accepting that civil authority governs issues concerning marriage and divorce is therefore a key factor in correctly interpreting Jesus' words. God is the ultimate ruler over all civil governments, whether they recognize Him as such or not. It is He that exalts and tears down nations. Governments will be exalted that are faithful to administer their designated purpose of restraining the immoral, sinful nature of man by punishing evildoers. God will also eventually tear down all governments that oppose Him and the establishment of His spiritual kingdom of righteousness and peace.

Jesus recognized that the Pharisees had civil authority and should be obeyed, although not followed. *"The teachers of the law and the Pharisees sit in Moses' seat. So you must obey them and do everything they tell you. But do not do what they do, for they do not practice what they preach"* (Matthew 23:2-3 NIV). Nowhere is Jesus recorded attempting to change civil legislation; nor does He speak concerning such. Jesus spoke prophetically concerning the attitudes of our hearts.

Jesus did not come to establish or change the Law. He did not come as a legislator, but as a prophet. Interpretations of the difficult passages concerning divorce must agree with these elements of the authorial context. If they do not, then the interpretations are in error. Jesus did not intend to change the Law of Moses, neither did He wish to speak legislatively, correcting civil law. Therefore He did not wish to repudiate the bill of divorce or declare marriage indissoluble; both of which would have been contrary to the Mosaic Law!

# Chapter XIII

# PUT AWAY

If Jesus did not intend to repudiate the bill of divorce, what did He mean by what He said? To begin answering this question, we will look at the meanings of the key words "put away" and "but." It will be helpful to review these passages as interpreted by the King James Version because of its wooden, literal style of translation, as opposed to modern English translations that are more fluid, dynamic, and interpretive. The specific words and word phrases under consideration are emboldened in the following quotes.

Matthew 5:31-32 (KJV)
*It hath been said, Whosoever* **shall put away** *his wife, let him give her a writing of divorcement:* **But** *I say unto you, That whosoever* **shall put away** *his wife, saving for the cause of fornication, causeth her to commit adultery: and whosoever shall marry her that is* **divorced** *committeth adultery.*

Matthew 19:3-9 (KJV)
*The Pharisees also came unto him, tempting him, and saying unto him, Is it lawful for a man* **to put away** *his wife for* **every cause**? *And he answered and said unto them, "Have ye not read, that he which made them at the beginning made them male and female, And said, For this cause shall a man leave father and mother, and shall cleave to his wife: and they twain shall be one flesh? ⁶Wherefore they are no more twain, but one flesh. What therefore God hath joined together, let not man put asunder." They say unto him, Why did Moses then command to give a writing of divorcement, and* **to put** *her*

*away? He saith unto them, "Moses, because of the hardness of your hearts, suffered you **to put away** your wives: but from the beginning it was not so. And I say unto you, Whosoever **shall put away** his wife, except it be for fornication, and shall marry another, committeth adultery: and whoso marrieth her which is **put away** doth commit adultery."*

Mark 10:2-12 (KJV)
*And the Pharisees came to him, and asked him, Is it lawful for a man **to put away** his wife? tempting him. And he answered and said unto them, What did Moses command you? And they said, Moses suffered to write a bill of divorcement, and **to put her away**. And Jesus answered and said unto them, For the hardness of your heart he wrote you this precept. But from the beginning of the creation God made them male and female. For this cause shall a man leave his father and mother, and cleave to his wife; And they twain shall be one flesh: so then they are no more twain, but one flesh. What therefore God hath joined together, let not man put asunder. And in the house his disciples asked him again of the same matter. And he saith unto them, Whosoever **shall put away** his wife, **and marry another**, committeth adultery against her. And **if a woman shall put away** her husband, and be married to another, she committeth adultery.*

Luke 16:18 (KJV)
*Whosoever **putteth away** his wife, **and marrieth** another, committeth adultery: and whosoever **marrieth** her that is **put away** from her husband committeth adultery.*

A key word in these difficult passages is the Greek word "**apŏluō**," translated as "put away" in the King James Version. Understanding the passages in Matthew and Luke depends upon the meaning of this word. Like any other word, it has a variety of meanings. Most are similar with slight nuancial differences. The best **interpretation** will be firmly founded upon the context (literary, cultural, and authorial). The following is from the *New Strong's Dictionary of Greek and Hebrew Words*.

630.   ἀπολύω **apŏluō**, *ap-ol-oo'-o;* from 575 and 3089; to *free* fully, i.e. (lit.) *relieve, release, dismiss* (refl. *depart*), or (fig.) *let die, pardon* or (spec.) *divorce:*— (let) depart, dismiss, divorce, forgive, let go, loose, put (send) away, release, set at liberty.[32]

**Apŏluo** can mean divorce; but dismiss, put away, let go, or desert are also viable interpretations. Concerning the difficult passage in Mark 10, in his commentary, *The Gospel of Mark*, William L. Lane says, "If the reading supported by the Western and Cesarean families of texts is correct, Jesus did not speak of divorce in verse 12, but of **desertion** and remarriage". (emphasis mine)[33]

For the last few centuries, Greek manuscripts of the New Testament have been divided into either three or four different families, dependant upon their textual characteristics and the analysis of the scholar. The three primary groups are the Western, Alexandrian, and Byzantine families of manuscripts. Some scholars add a fourth called the Cesarean. Textual criticism is a science and art unto itself and is well beyond the scope of this book, but it is helpful to note that "desertion" is a viable interpretation of "**apŏluō**" and one supported by a significant number of manuscripts.

Concerning the difficult passages in Matthew 5:31-32 ethnologist and Aramaic language expert, George M. Lamsa, B. A., wrote in his book "Gospel Light,"

> It is very important to know that the Eastern text in reference to this verse uses two Aramaic words whereas Western texts use only one. One word is **nishbook** which means to leave, and the other is **nishry** which means to divorce. At the present day, if a man marries a woman who is left, both man and woman are excommunicated from the church. But if a woman who has been left by her husband obtains a decree of **shiriana**, divorce, which means the **loosening of the bond**, she is allowed to marry again and the marriage is lawful. (emphasis mine)[34]

Some scholars believe that parts of the New Testament, like Matthew, were actually written in Aramaic and then translated into Greek, the international language of the day. Whether or not this is true is not extremely significant to this discourse; but it is significant to note that the mother tongue of the writers of the New Testament (except for Luke) was Aramaic; and Jesus would more than likely have spoken these passages in Aramaic. Therefore, it is helpful to study the Aramaic text to gain a fuller understanding of any New Testament passage, especially the Gospels. The following are quotes from Lamsa's translation of the Bible, *"The Holy Bible From Ancient Eastern Manuscripts: Containing the Old and New Testaments, translated from the Peshitta, the Authorized Bible of the Church of the East."* I have again emboldened the words that are significant to our immediate discussion.

Matthew 5:31-32 (AEM)
*It has been said that whoever divorces his wife, must give her the divorce papers. But I say to you that whoever **divorces** his wife, except for fornication, causes her to commit adultery; and whoever marries a woman who is **separated but not divorced**, commits adultery.*

Matthew 19:8-9 (AEM)
*He said to them, "Moses, considering the hardness of your heart, gave you permission to **divorce** your wives; but from the beginning it was not so. But I say to you, whoever **leaves** his wife without a charge of adultery and marries another commits adultery; and he who marries a woman thus **separated** commits adultery."*

Luke 16:18 (AEM)
*He who **divorces** his wife and marries another commits adultery; and he who marries the one who is **illegally separated** commits adultery.*

Previously, we noted in our discussion of Deuteronomy 24:1 that in biblical times in the Middle East if a wife was "put away," but not given a bill of divorce, any subsequent "marriages" were considered illegitimate and adulterous. A Biblical example of this is the illegitimate marriage between Palti and Michal (King David's wife). A woman was bound under civil law to her husband though he had abandoned her or expelled her from his household; and women did not have the civil right to divorce their husbands. A certificate of divorce enabled an abandoned wife to marry another man without legal or social repercussions. If husbands abandoned their wives, they were commanded to give their wives bills of divorce freeing them to remarry, rather than relegating them to lives of poverty, adultery, or even prostitution. Illegal separation (desertion without a legally recognized divorce) was a serious problem for their society.

"Desertion" (as in illegal separation) and "divorce" are both viable translations of the Greek word "apŏluō." In order to ascertain Jesus' intended meaning, we are thus dependant upon the cultural, literary, and authorial context of the passages in question. Interpreting "apŏluo" as "divorce" raises several questions and is difficult, if not impossible to reconcile with the character of Christ, His role as a prophet, and His love, mercy, and forgiveness that He consistently exhibited–the authorial context. It also does not fit the cultural context, because the viability of divorce was never questioned. On the other hand, desertion, illegal separation, and, more specifically, "expulsion without a bill of divorce" makes sense in light of the authorial and cultural context. When applied to the difficult passages under our examination, this one textual consideration effectively makes these difficult passages, no longer difficult, as we will see!

SUBJUNCTIVE MOOD OF THE VERB " Gamĕo "

Another consideration that is important for correctly interpreting these difficult passages is the Greek text subjunctive mood of "marries." Larry W. Hurtado notes in His commentary on Mark concerning Mark 10: 11 & 12, "The situation in view here is a man divorcing his wife in order to be free to marry another, or a wife doing the same to her husband".[35] (emphasis mine) This radically challenges the "plain" meaning of the text.

The subjunctive "mood" in the Greek text of "put away, apŏluō," and "marries, gamĕō," is what suggests this interpretation. "The subjunctive mood is the mood of probability. It is the mood of contingency, generally indicated by words such as 'may,' 'might,' or 'should.'"[36] Therefore another viable translation of these difficult passages is that the man puts away his wife in order to be free to marry another woman, emphasizing the motive for the action. Surprisingly, this is even brought out in a couple of modern translations.

Matthew 19:9 (CEV)
*I say that if your wife has not committed some terrible sexual sin, you must not divorce her **to marry** someone else. If you do, you are unfaithful. (emphasis mine)*

Mark 10:11-12 (The Message by Eugene H. Peterson)
*When they were back home, the disciple brought it up again. Jesus gave it to them straight: "A man who divorces his wife **so he can marry** someone else commits adultery against her. And a woman who divorces her husband **so she can marry** someone else commits adultery." (emphasis mine)*

If a man divorces his wife in order to marry another woman, he commits adultery. Well, that makes sense! This dynamically changes the meaning of this passage and is similar to Jesus' other statement concerning adultery, *"I say to you that whoever looks at a woman to lust for her has already committed adultery with her in his heart" (Matthew 5:28 NKJV).*

## THE CONJUNCTION " Dĕ "

A small, yet significant, word in these difficult passages is the Greek word "δέ **dĕ**, *deh"* which can be translated as *"and, but, also,* or *moreover."* The context determines the translation. The English word "but" has the connotation of drawing a contrast between contradicting concepts, statements, or philosophies. Whereas, the words *"and, also,* or *moreover"* have different connotations. *"And"* and *"also"* draw attention to similarities. *"Moreover"* affirms the first statement and implies the second statement goes beyond the first, being greater or more explicit in some dimension. The literary and authorial contexts of these passages lend themselves to the use of *"moreover,"* as opposed to *"but."* Jesus repeatedly stated that He did not disagree with the Mosaic Law. Jesus would have endorsed and reaffirmed the Law speaking concerning the issue of the heart or the social problem that made the law necessary. "Moreover" is thus a better translation of "**dĕ**" in the difficult passages.

TRANSLATION OF " Pŏrnĕiă "

A phrase unique to the passages in Matthew is the exception clause concerning fornication (Matthew 5:31 & 19:9). *"Fornication"* in Greek is πορνεία **pŏrnĕia,** *por-ni'-ah.* It is a broad term commonly used to reference a wide range of illicit, immoral, and unlawful sexual acts and/or relationships including adultery involving a married person or persons, fornication involving singles, homosexuality, lesbianism, and intercourse with close relatives or animals. Like any other word with multiple meanings, the translation of **pŏrnĕia** is dependent upon the immediate literary context. In the difficult passages in Matthew, is it best translated as sexual intercourse before marriage, incest, adultery, bestiality, homosexuality, lesbianism, or unlawful immoral relationships?

Although several modern versions translate **pŏrnĕia** in these passages as adultery, it is significant to note that the specific word for adultery, μοιχεία **mŏichĕia,** *moy-khi'-ah,* is not used though used elsewhere in the passage. If the immediate context of the passage concerned acceptable reasons for divorce, **mŏichĕia** would have been a better and more natural term to use. However, the context of the passage in Matthew 19 is about the Any Matter, no-fault divorce system, and an argumentative question concerning the reason for Moses' endorsement of the bill of divorce. The context does not concern acceptable reasons for divorce. Thus **mŏichĕia** was not used and adultery is not a good translation of **pŏrnĕia** in Matthew's exception clauses.

Another interpretation often espoused is that **pŏrnĕia** refers to unfaithfulness before the wedding, during the "engagement" period. This is also an incorrect interpretation because in Hebraic Near-Eastern first century culture this unfaithfulness would have been considered adultery and would require a certificate of divorce to break the existing marriage covenant. Recall the story of Mary, the mother of Jesus. Although she and Joseph had never been intimate, when she was found to be with child, Joseph was going to put her away quietly using the Any Matter divorce procedure because it appeared that she had committed adultery. In like manner, the more specific word for adultery, **mŏichĕia** would have been a more natural fit *if* Jesus were speaking in Matthew 5 or 19 of unfaithfulness during what we would call the engagement period. Unfaithfulness during the "engagement" period is thus an interpretation that is read into the text, rather than coming from the context—a bad procedure for interpretation.

In the context of the "Any Matter" divorce debate, it has also been argued that the Greek word **pŏrnĕia** (fornication) is a translation of the Hebraic word **'ervâh** (indecency) or **'ervâh dâbâr** (a matter of indecency) as mentioned in Deuteronomy 24:1. Dr. David Instone-Brewer supports this interpretation. He states that,

> In conclusion, contemporary Jews would have mentally added something like this exception, whether it was present or not. They would either have added "except for valid grounds" (if they were thinking of divorce in general) or they would have added "except for indecency" (if they were thinking just about Deuteronomy 24:1). In Matthew the clause "except for indecency" was used because the whole incident, as he reported it, is concerned with the debate about Deuteronomy 24:1.[37]

The initial question of the Pharisees in Matthew 19:3 did concern Deuteronomy 24:1, but Jesus' following response expands the discussion to marriage and divorce in general. One must also take into consideration that the divorce mentioned in Deuteronomy 24:1 was likely for legitimate, morally acceptable reasons; whereas the second divorce mentioned in Deuteronomy 24:3 was a hateful divorce–one based on selfish reasons and not precipitated by a morally acceptable reason. Jesus would have understood this distinction and could therefore have been alluding to the difference between a divorce based on legitimate reasons, and one based on illegitimate reasons. However, this interpretation also incorrectly assumes that Jesus is speaking of acceptable reasons for divorce. Neither is He discussing the viability of divorce. He is explaining the reason for the bill of divorce. Therefore neither "except for valid grounds" or "except for indecency" fits well the immediate literary context or the authorial context.

The *New American Standard Bible* and the *Catholic New American Bible* translates "except for **pŏrnĕia**" as "**unless the marriage is unlawful.**"

Another viable interpretation is **"except for unlawful relationships."** Considering the immediate literary context, this translation is the best. In Matthew 19, Jesus explains why Moses endorsed the bill of divorce. The purpose of the bill of divorce was to free an abandoned wife to remarry and remain in that marriage without negative social or legal ramifications, or the fear of her first husband reclaiming her years later (as with King David and Michal). If a relationship is not lawful, it does not need a bill of divorce in order to break the relationship.

"Except for unlawful relationships" also dynamically fits the immediate geo-political context of the confrontation between the Pharisees and Jesus. The episode in Matthew 19 & Mark 10 took place in Herod's territory. Thus Jesus could have been alluding to what Herod needed to do, or not to do, concerning his immoral and illegal relationship with Herodias. Although Herodias and Herod were living together like husband and wife, Herodias was still legally married to Phillip, Herod's brother. Herod needed to put away Herodias, but no certificate of divorce was necessary because they were not legally married.

"Except for unlawful relationships" also readily speaks to immoral and illegal relationships of today. If a couple is just living together, they need to either separate or get married in order to receive more of God's blessing in their lives and relationship.

# Chapter XIV
## SERMON ON THE MOUNT

The literary context includes the immediately preceding and following passages, the style of the passage (parable, overstatement, narrative, didactic, apocalyptic, etc.), its placement in the outline of the book, the book's overall message, target audience, etc. A book could be written concerning the literary context of each of the four passages that Jesus speaks concerning divorce. Here, we will only note a few elements of each. This will give us more than enough information to distill a well informed contextually based interpretation of Jesus' words. At the end of each of the discourses concerning the literary context of each of the difficult passages, the passages will be interpreted based on a combination of the information we have discussed concerning the historical, cultural, authorial, and literary context.

Two of the difficult passages of Jesus concerning divorce are in Matthew. It is commonly accepted among scholars that Matthew was written to the Jew, persuading him that Jesus is the Messiah, the anointed Son of David who would inaugurate a new era of God's Kingdom on earth. Jesus is the promised one of the house of David, the Savior of the world! Matthew goes to great lengths to validate for the Hebrew, Jesus' ministry and mission, recording Jesus' fulfillment of nine Messianic prophesies and the testimonies of those who recognized Jesus as the Messiah, the Son of David.

One of the few, if not the only, consistent element of the literary context of all four difficult passages on divorce is Jesus' opposition of the Pharisees. This is vital to understanding Jesus' words. As one reads through the Gospels, it is evident that in the short three years of Jesus' public ministry there is a rapid escalation of tension and animosity between Jesus and the Pharisees. The Pharisees eventually sought Jesus' death, and Jesus openly denounced the Pharisees and teachers of the Law as hypocritical, judgmental leaders that do not know God, calling them sons of Satan.

The difficult passage in Matthew 5:31-32 is part of the "Sermon on the Mount" (Matthew 5-7). In Matthew 5:20 Jesus says, *"For I tell you that unless your righteousness surpasses that of the Pharisees and the teachers of the law, you will certainly not enter the kingdom of heaven."* This is a key verse in understanding a large portion of the Sermon on the Mount, for in the verses following Matthew 5:20, Jesus addresses several of the errant teachings, bad attitudes, and wrong motives of the hypocritical religious leaders of His day, the Pharisees. Divorce fit this category and was one topic Jesus briefly addressed and Matthew was inspired to record in this literary context. Let us look at a few of the other things Jesus addresses in the Sermon on the Mount.

Jesus taught men not to look lustfully at a women (Matthew 5:27 & 28); doing so was tantamount to adultery. Regarding murder, Jesus taught us to keep short accounts and not let anger and resentment build in our relationships, equating hatred with murder (Matthew 5:21–24). Concerning swearing oaths, He taught us to be people of integrity and thus not need to swear because our word is our bond, and not to be deceptive by saying something that is technically correct, but deceptive none the less (Matthew 5:33-37).

In Matthew 6:1-4 Jesus says not to be like the hypocrites when doing good things for others. When they do something good, they make a show of it, getting everyone's attention so that others will think good of them. Our motivation should be different; it should be selfless; and when possible, we need to do things in secret, helping to preserve the dignity of those we serve.

Concerning prayer (6:5-15) and fasting (6:16-18), we are not to be like the hypocrites that make an outward show of their piety and devotion to God, although they don't know God or have a personal relationship with Him. We must know God personally and intimately. We should grow in our relationship with Him in the secret place of our heart, a private place of devotion to Him where we can be intimate with Him and He with us. There, He can reveal to us, Himself, and bring cleansing and healing to the issues of uncleanness and wickedness in our hearts, delivering us from our own personal demons.

The Sermon on the Mount is about the motives of the heart and having a personal relationship with God, as opposed to a religious ritual. It makes sense that Jesus' comments on divorce would follow this pattern. In the following personal amplified version, I have taken into account the literary, cultural, and authorial context previously discussed. Rather than translating "apŏluō" as "put away," I have elected to translate it as "desertion" because it has a stronger negative connotation.

Matthew 5:31-32 (Personal Amplified Translation)
*It has been said, "Anyone who expels or deserts his wife should give her a bill of divorce (so that she is free to marry another without negative social or legal ramifications). Moreover, I say to you that, except for unlawful relationships or marriages, anyone who expels or deserts his wife (without giving her a bill of divorce) causes her to commit adultery (because she is still legally bound to him and cannot legally marry another). And anyone that marries a woman that has been deserted (without having been given a bill of divorce) commits adultery (because she is still legally bound to her husband).*

This "sounds" like something Jesus would say! More importantly, it underscores His endorsement of the Law, reveals His concern for the oppressed, would have helped bring clarity concerning the issue of divorce, uncovers the Spirit behind the Law, and can bring a righteous conviction to the hearer in any culture. More than likely, this was the tag line of an extended discussion concerning divorce.

The traditional "plain" interpretation in no way sounds like something Jesus would say! Worse, it implies that Jesus disagreed with the Law, confuses the issue of marriage and divorce, and condemns many people (divorcées) to lives of hopelessness—the antithesis of the Gospel. Should we then accept the "plain" meaning of the text, or a contextually based interpretation?

# *Chapter XV*
# CONFRONTING THE PHARISEES

The immediate literary context of the difficult passage about divorce in Matthew 19:8-9 is a story about a verbal confrontation between Jesus and the Pharisees. Verse 3 notes that the Pharisees' purpose in asking Jesus about the "Any Matter" divorce was to trap Him in some way. The Pharisees probably hoped to engage Jesus in debate, find some reason to denounce Him, and cause Him to lose respect among the people. More than likely, they also intended to position Jesus against Herod and Herodias, hoping that He would be beheaded like John the Baptist was for denouncing their immoral and illegal relationship.

Understanding this, Jesus responded *"Have ye not read, that he which made them at the beginning made them male and female, And said, For this cause shall a man leave father and mother, and shall cleave to his wife: and they twain shall be one flesh? Wherefore they are no more twain, but one flesh. What therefore God hath joined together, let not man put asunder"* (Matthew 19:4-6 KJV).

To their inquiry about the "Any Matter" divorce, Jesus strongly affirmed the divine ideal for marriage as a monogamous, faithful, life-long union of a man and woman in an interdependent familial relationship that should not be broken apart by man. He affirmed that God is vitally interested in the stability of marital relationships and families. Marriage is much more than just a means of having children or lawfully fulfilling one's sexual passion; marriage is an institution ordained by God and should be treated as such. It is

164 GOD IS A DIVORCÉ TOO!

as if Jesus is saying, *"Why strain out gnats, arguing over divorce legislation and proceedings? You should be discussing how important marriage is and how to help marriages endure."*

Jesus' words, empowered by the Holy Spirit, would have brought tremendous conviction to all that heard it and would have expanded the people's respect for Jesus—exactly the opposite results of what the Pharisees desired. In an effort not to allow Jesus to evade the debate on the viability of the "Any Matter" divorce civil legislation, they pressed Him further, argumentatively asking, *"Why did Moses then command to give a writing of divorcement, and to put her away?"*

Jesus responded, *"Moses, because of the hardness of your hearts, suffered you to put away your wives: but from the beginning it was not so."* Based on Jesus' relationship with and stated endorsement of the Law of Moses, we must assume that Jesus is not disagreeing with the Law of Moses, but endorsing it and explaining the reason for the law. Therefore, Jesus is saying that Moses (under the inspiration of God) allowed divorce because of mankind's hardness of heart, but from creation God never intended for people to treat their spouses so badly as to require divorce.

Immediately following the difficult passage in verse nine, Matthew records the disciples' response, *"If such is the case of a man with his wife, it is better not to marry"* (NKJV). Many commentaries make much over this passage. It is assumed that Jesus' statement concerning marriage made such a strong impression upon the disciples that they had a radical reaction, moving toward the opposite extreme, celibacy. Based on the traditional doctrine of marriage and divorce, this passage is interpreted as implying that the disciples were saying that celibacy is better than marriage because a person might be stuck married to someone that proves to be a terrible spouse. However, the mood of the passage could have been very different, and thus support an entirely different interpretation.

Rather than assuming that the disciples are exhibiting an extreme reaction to what Jesus said, what if they were simply processing the information and weighing the various options and implications of what Jesus said, with celibacy being the most extreme option. It is significant to note that in Mark's account this is the mood of the disciples' response to what Jesus said, that of a more discursive and contemplative mood, rather than a reactionary mood. If this was the case, then the disciples' statement concerning celibacy is more of a question, than an assertion. Could it be that the disciples even spoke of celibacy sarcastically? Yes, that is also a possible way to interpret the mood of the disciples.

What commentaries often fail to mention is the radical nature of Jesus' reply to their question/statement/joke concerning celibacy. To procreate was considered one of the primary "laws" of the Torah. It was the first command of God to mankind; *"And God blessed them, and God said unto them, Be fruitful, and multiply, and replenish the earth,"* (Genesis 1:28a KJV). To get married and have children was a Jewish *social* and even a *religious* expectation. People recognized that some times, men were born eunuchs or became eunuchs due to an accident or the aggression of others. However, to choose to become a eunuch for the sake of the Kingdom of God was a radical, anti-traditional concept for the Jew.

Before we translate the difficult passage in verse nine let us look at the extended literary context of the Matthew 19 passage on divorce. Immediately preceding Jesus' confrontation with the Pharisees concerning the "Any Matter" divorce, Mathew records the 'Parable of the Unmerciful Servant' (Matthew 18:21-35). A man owed his king millions of dollars. The king ordered that the man, his wife, children, and all that he owned to be sold in order to pay the debt. The servant begged for mercy and an extension of time to repay the debt. The king had pity on the man, completely forgiving him the debt.

After the man left the king, he came across a man that owed him a few dollars and demanded payment. This man also begged for an extension. The first man threw his fellow servant into prison until he could pay the debt. Upon hearing of this, the king called back the servant whom he had forgiven and said, *"You wicked servant. I cancelled all that debt of yours because you begged me to. Shouldn't you have had mercy on your fellow servant just as I had on you"* (Matthew 18:32-33). The king then threw the man in jail to be tortured until he could repay all that he owed the king. Jesus then says, *"This is how my heavenly Father will treat each of you unless you forgive your brother from your heart"* (Matthew 18:35 NIV). It is upon this foundational literary context of forgiveness, that Matthew records Jesus' confrontation with the Pharisees over divorce. We then are encouraged to understand the difficult passage about divorce based upon the foundation of the forgiveness that one finds in the person of Christ and in the Gospel.

Immediately following the Matthew 19 section on divorce, as in Mark 10, is the famous passage of Jesus rebuking His disciples for not allowing the children to come to Him. *"But Jesus said, 'Let the little children come to Me, and do not forbid them; for of such is the kingdom of heaven'"* (Matthew 19:14 NKJV). This passage speaks of unconditional and undeserved acceptance and compassion. We come to Jesus based on His goodness, compassion, and acceptance, not based on who we are or what we can bring to Him. Thus the difficult meaty passage concerning divorce is sandwiched between the bread of forgiveness and unmerited acceptance–WOW! In the same way, our understanding of divorce needs to be tempered by the forgiveness and grace, unmerited acceptance, of God.

Based upon the extended and immediate literary context, as well as upon the cultural and authorial context, let us now interpret Matthew 19:7-9.

Matthew 19:7-9 (Personal Amplified Translation)
*The Pharisees then argumentatively said to Jesus, "If marriage is a union established and supported by God, then why did Moses command us to give our wives divorce papers and expel them from our homes?" Jesus replied, "First of all, Moses did not command you to desert your wives, but allowed you to do so. God never intended for people to become so cruel and hard-hearted towards their spouses as to make divorce necessary. Furthermore, except for unlawful marriages and relationships, whoever divorces his wife, in order to marry another, commits adultery. And Moses instructed you to give your wives divorce papers (if you are so hard-hearted as to desert them) because whoever marries a woman that has been deserted but not divorced, commits adultery, because she is still legally bound to her husband.*

This sounds like something that Jesus would say. Moreover, it underscores His endorsement of the Law, reveals His concern for the oppressed, would have helped bring clarity concerning the issue of divorce (making it a matter of the heart before God), uncovers the Spirit of and reason behind the Law of Moses, and brings a righteous conviction to us today. On the other hand, the "plain" interpretation in no way sounds like something Jesus would say! Worse, it implies that Jesus disagreed with the Law, confuses the issue of marriage and divorce, and condemns many people (divorcées) to lives of hopelessness–the antithesis of the Gospel.

# Chapter XVI
# THE FAITHFUL FATHER

In Chapter 16, Luke briefly mentions Jesus' words concerning "putting away." Once again though, it is in the context of Jesus confronting the Pharisees. In Luke 15, Jesus tells the Parables of the Lost Sheep, the Parable of the Lost Coin, and the Parable of the Lost Son (the Prodigal Son). All three of these parables highlight the value of mankind to God and His desire for the salvation of all who are lost. God, in the Parable of the Lost Sheep, is the Good Shepherd that forsakes all to search out and find those who are lost from His presence and protection (Luke 15:4-7). In the Parable of the Lost Coin, God is the woman who refuses to give up until she finds the gold coin that she has lost (Luke 15:8-10). God is also the loving father who faithfully embraces the rebellious son that returns home in the Parable of the Lost Son. This faithful father (God) even lovingly corrects the son who had a wrong and selfish attitude (the Pharisees) towards the returning brother (sinners). God is a faithful loving father (Luke 15:11-32). The Pharisees, on the other hand, thought evil of Jesus because he embraced, forgave, accepted, and fellowshipped with sinners (Luke 15:2).

Continuing His rebuke of the Pharisees, in Luke 16:1-13, Jesus tells the Parable of the Unjust Steward who was commended for his shrewdness although his actions were dishonest. Jesus said to the Pharisees, *"You are the ones who justify yourselves in the eyes of men, but God knows your hearts. What is highly valued among men is detestable in God's sight"* (Luke 16:14-15). Can you hear the anger and frustration in His voice? Nothing angered

Jesus more than the hypocritical, self-righteous, judgmental attitudes, and demonic teachings of the Pharisees.

Then in Luke 16:19-31 Jesus tells the story of the Rich Man and Lazarus. This further challenged some of the foundational beliefs of the Pharisees. Prosperity was not necessarily a sign of being right with God; nor was poverty always an indication of God's displeasure. What is important is to be generous and good to your fellow man, without being judgmental.

In Luke 16:16 Jesus affirms that *"The Law and the Prophets were proclaimed until John. Since that time, the good news of the kingdom of God is being preached, and everyone is forcing his way into it."* Notice that Jesus draws a contrast between the proclamation of the Mosaic Law and the Prophets, with the preaching of the Gospel, the good news of the kingdom of God. Adherence to law, legalism was a foundational life philosophy for the Pharisees, but Jesus infers that it is not through adherence to the law, even the Law of Moses, but through faith in the Gospel that people gain access to the Kingdom of God.

Jesus then affirms the continued importance of the Law by saying, *"It is easier for heaven and earth to disappear than for the least stroke of a pen to drop out of the Law"* (Luke 16:17). The Law was given to reveal our need for God, not to keep us from God, to teach us how to live, not to condemn us. Faith in and relationship with God predates reception of the Law. In the same way, in our lives, faith in and relationship with God should be the foundation for faithful living in Christ and fulfilling the Law. This verse also dispels the concept that Jesus disagreed in any way with the Mosaic Law concerning divorce. Immediately following this verse, and within the literary context of God's love for mankind, Luke briefly notes Jesus' address concerning a man putting away his wife.

Luke 16:18 is set against the prevailing religious, hypocritical, judgmental, and condemning attitude and doctrine of the Pharisees, the hypocritical religious leaders of that day. It needs to be interpreted and understood in that literary context. It must also communicate a message of conviction, forgiveness, and hope; anything less is not the Gospel.

Based upon the extended and immediate literary context, as well as upon the cultural and authorial context previously discussed, let us now interpret Luke 16:18.

Luke 16:18 (Personal Amplified Translation)
*Whoever divorces his wife in order to marry another, commits adultery: and whoever marries a woman who is deserted by her husband (but not given a bill of divorce) commits adultery (because she is still legally bound to her husband).*

This interpretation fits well the literary, cultural, and authorial context. Remember that a "text" without a "context" is a "pretext"–an assumed meaning that often hides the author's true intentions. The "plain" meaning is thus a "pretext" and effectively hides the authorial intent. However, a contextually based translation has the potential of communicating more closely what the author meant.

In this one verse, Luke distills Jesus' teaching concerning divorce. If a man divorces his wife for selfish reasons, in order to marry another, it is tantamount to adultery! Furthermore, the purpose of the bill of divorce was to free an abandoned woman to marry again without fear of negative civil, religious, or social sanctions.

# Chapter XVII
# A TEACHABLE MOMENT

*"A man who divorces his wife **so he can marry** someone else commits adultery against her. And a woman who divorces her husband **so she can marry** someone else commits adultery"* (Mark 10:12 The Message). This makes sense and sounds like something that Jesus would say, much more so than the traditional interpretation, which says, *"Whoever divorces his wife **and marries** another commits adultery against her. And if a woman divorces her husband **and marries** another, she commits adultery"* (Mark 10:11-12 NKJV). But is the quote from *The Message* a viable interpretation? Absolutely!

Previously we discussed the implications of the subjunctive mood of the verbs "put away, **apŏluō**," and "marries, **gaměō**." Therefore, either interpretation, "divorces so that he can marry," or "divorces and marries" is viable. We are then dependent upon the context to properly translate the verse. "Divorce + marries = adultery" does not fit a biblical understanding of divorce, nor does it fit the character of Christ, or sound like something that He would say. However, "divorces **so that** he can marry," fits the context and character of Christ. It makes sense and sounds like something that Jesus would say. And as we shall see, it especially fits well the literary context of Mark.

Mark 10 records the same encounter with the Pharisees as the one in Matthew 19 although with significant variations. Both passages are set in the same location in the region of Judea across the Jordan from Galilee, Herod's territory. Jesus has left Capernum in Galilee and crowds of people have followed Him to the new location. The major difference between the two accounts is seen in that Matthew focused on Jesus' confrontation with the Pharisees. Whereas, Mark divided the passage between the confrontation with the Pharisees and a subsequent teaching session with the disciples. Apparently, this was an extended conversation of which we only have a little recorded.

Mark 10 begins with the Pharisees asking Jesus about divorce. Jesus responds with a question concerning Moses' command. The Pharisees reply mentioning the bill of divorce. Jesus responds denouncing the Pharisees for their hard-heartedness, emphasizing that it was due to such hard-heartedness that Moses wrote the law of divorce. Without questioning, much less disagreeing with the Law of Moses, Jesus then strongly affirms the divine ideal of marriage. Mark then closes the discussion with the Pharisees and separates out the difficult passage, putting it in a teaching context with the disciples.

It is widely accepted among biblical scholars that Matthew wrote with a Jewish audience in mind, and Mark wrote to a Roman audience. Matthew focused on Jesus' encounter with the Pharisees over the "Any Matter" divorce, an important and widely discussed topic among the Jews. Mark shortens the encounter with the Pharisees, not mentioning the Any Matter divorce debate or the "except for unlawful relationships" clause. Furthermore, the difficult passage in Mark is not addressed to the Pharisees, but later to the disciples in a separate location. In Mark, Jesus drew no distinction between a man divorcing his wife, and a woman divorcing her husband. Whereas, Matthew does not reference a woman divorcing her husband, but does mention a man marrying a woman who has been put away but not legally divorced.

Why are there such significant differences between Mark's account and Matthew's? Mark's Roman audience would have no knowledge concerning the culturally specific Jewish "Any Matter" divorce debate. Thus, there would have been no need to broach that subject for a Roman audience. In fact, without an extensive explanation, it would have been meaningless to them and could have caused much confusion, like the passage in Matthew has for the last 1900 years for non-Jewish readers. Furthermore, in Greco-Roman culture, women were almost equal to men concerning the right of divorce. Either the husband or the wife could enact divorce simply by leaving, requiring no civil documentation or intervention at all.

Mark clearly wrote with his Roman audience in mind. Mark emphasized that if a person divorces his/her spouse **in order to** marry another, it was as bad as adultery. The motive of the heart was paramount. Regardless of the apparent "reason" for divorce, if a person's primary motive is selfish, that person commits adultery against his spouse.

Notice that Jesus does not qualify his statement that a man commits adultery if he divorces his wife in order to marry another woman. What if the wife has physically committed adultery? Does the husband not have a moral right to divorce her <u>so that</u> he can marry someone else? Apparently not! What if the husband is unkind and uncaring, bordering on emotional neglect or abuse? The wife's needs are not being met. May she divorce him <u>so that</u> she can find someone else? No! If the motive of the divorce is selfish, then the woman sins against her husband and their marriage covenant, which is tantamount to adultery.

Does this mean that there is no such thing as a just divorce? Obviously not! If a man divorces his spouse, it should be motivated out of love and non-selfishness. Divorce, motivated by love, how can that be? God, motivated by His love for his wife, Israel, divorced her. God excluded her from His protection, provision, pastoral care, and intimacy with Him so that she might repent from her destructive lifestyle! He allowed her to be taken away into captivity, holding her accountable for her adultery, hoping that she would repent, and thus teaching others that such blatant evil and disregard for his covenant of love with them would not be tolerated. In the same way, we are called to walk in forgiveness with our spouses. If we do divorce, the primary motive needs to be love for our spouse and our children. This might seem incongruent, but love is not only exhibited in forgiveness, but also in accountability and discipline. <u>Mark's message is thus a prophetic call to a radical purity of heart in regards to marriage and especially in regards to divorce.</u>

The following Personal Amplified Translation takes into consideration: the cultural meaning of "one flesh," Jesus' agreement with Moses, His prophetic ministry concerning the issues of the heart, Mark's Roman audience, and the subjunctive mood of the verbs divorce and marry. It also attempts to express Jesus' passion concerning this topic and His opposition of the Pharisees.

Mark 10:2-12 (Personal Amplified Translation)
*The Pharisees came to Jesus with ill will to trap Him in His words, asking, "Is divorce lawful?" And Jesus answered, "What did Moses command you?" They replied, "Moses permitted us to give them divorce papers and expel them from our households."*

*But Jesus responded, "Because of the hardness of your hearts, Moses established this legislation concerning divorce, but from the beginning of creation God never intended for men to divorce their wives and treat them so badly. God made mankind, male and female and instructed the man to leave his father and mother, and purposefully build with his wife a new family—the foundation of social order. They should no longer to be considered two totally separate individuals, but are united into one interdependent family relationship. And what God has yoked together, man should not bust apart!"*

*Later, in the house where they were staying, His disciples asked Him further about divorce. So Jesus said to them, "Whoever divorces his wife in order to marry another commits adultery against her. And if a woman divorces her husband in order to marry another, she commits adultery."*

Jesus effectively rebuked the Pharisees, and then went on to teach the disciples concerning the motive behind divorce. Though a man divorces his wife for a legally and morally acceptable reason like adultery, if he did so in order to marry another, he commits adultery too. Jesus went beyond outward appearance and civil law, prophetically speaking about the motive of the heart.

Having discussed the immediate literary context of the difficult passage in Mark 10:11-12, let us expand our examination. Setting aside the geographical changes in location that Mark records, it is interesting that just prior to Mark's passage on divorce is a warning about how we (especially religious leaders) should treat people, particularly children, and people with child-like faith. *"But if anyone causes one of these little ones who trusts in me to lose faith, it would be better for that person to be thrown into the sea with a large millstone tied around the neck"* (Mark 9:42 NLT).

Immediately following the passage on divorce, Jesus rebukes the disciples for hindering the little children from coming to Him.

> *Some people brought their little children to Jesus so he could touch them, but his followers told them to stop. When Jesus saw this, he was upset and said to them, "Let the little children come to me. Don't stop them, because the kingdom of God belongs to people who are like these children. I tell you the truth, you must accept the kingdom of God as if you were a little child, or you will never enter it." Then Jesus took the children in his arms, put his hands on them, and blessed them* (Mark 10:13-16 NCV).

Children are important to Jesus, and there is certainly no other institution more important to their spiritual, emotional, physical, and social health than the family! Statistical research increasingly confirms this. Children of divorce have a higher probability of divorce themselves. They do not do as well in school. They are more prone to become addicted to alcohol and drugs. Children of divorce typically live below the poverty line and have a higher propensity for premarital sex and thus sexually transmitted diseases and pregnancy outside of marriage. Is it any wonder that Jesus would call everyone to a high standard concerning marriage, fidelity, and divorce, far beyond what is controllable via civil legislation, much less ecclesiastical excommunication? Jesus understood how devastating divorce is for children.

What a multi-sided message! To religious leaders it says, *"Be careful about the rules and regulations that you put on people. They must not hinder people from coming to God in child-like faith."* To the divorcée it says, *"Do not let so-called religious leaders hinder you from coming to Jesus. Touch Him, and He will bring healing into your life."* To the married person it says, *"You need to have a holy reverence for God, especially in regards to your marriage. If your actions cause your spouse or your children to lose their faith, it would be better for you that someone killed you before committing such a sin. God has a tremendous interest in your marriage and your children. He loves you; and if you will only come to Him in child-like faith, He will move heaven and earth to help you make a go of it!"*

# Chapter XVIII
# A RADICAL PARADIGM SHIFT

The personal amplified translations of Jesus' words on divorce in the previous four chapters fit well their literary contexts. Jesus is revealed as supporting and clarifying the Mosaic Law, and prophetically speaking concerning the issues of the heart that made the Law of divorce necessary, rather than contradicting and much less repudiating it. These translations negate the nonsensical questions and conjectures raised by the "plain" meaning of the traditional interpretation or modern translations. They fit well the cultural context, and most importantly, they line up with the revealed character of Jesus—His grace, mercy, forgiveness, concern for the oppressed, and opposition of hypocritical religious oppression.

Something these interpretations do not bring out is the radical paradigm shift required by Jesus' words about a husband committing adultery against his wife. William L. Lane in his commentary on Mark, says,

> "According to rabbinical law, a man could commit adultery against another married man by seducing his wife (Duet. 22:13-19); and a wife could commit adultery against her husband by infidelity, but a husband could not be said to commit adultery against his wife. This sharp intensifying of the concept of adultery had the effect of elevating the status of the wife to the same dignity as her husband and placed the husband under an obligation of fidelity."[38] (emphasis mine)

It is difficult in our culture today to fully appreciate the impact of what

Jesus said. In the first century, women were under severe social and religious pressure to be sexually pure, especially in Jewish communities. On the other hand, though married, men were under little, if any, social or religious pressure to not indulge their sexual appetites through harlots, singles, or divorcées.

Adultery was considered a heinous crime punishable by death. It was one of the Ten Commandments actually written by the finger of God (Exodus 31:18, Deuteronomy 4:18, Exodus 20:1-17). Hypocritically, this Law was almost exclusively applied to women. To be branded an adulteress was to become an outcast of society. Men were rarely, if ever, branded adulterers. An example of this is when the Pharisees brought Jesus a woman caught in the act of adultery, but the man caught with her was not charged (John 8:1-11). It is difficult for us to appreciate the radical paradigm shift required by Jesus holding husbands accountable for the way they treat their wives.

Jesus' words required men to rethink their relationships with their wives. In the same way, a contextually based interpretation of Jesus' words requires us to rethink our understanding of marriage, divorce, and remarriage. For example, you have probably heard specific reasons for divorce described as "scriptural" or "unscriptural." This wording implies that some reasons for divorce are biblically acceptable and others are not. However, the Bible DOES NOT establish specific acceptable or non-acceptable reasons for divorce! God allows divorce because of the hardness of heart in mankind, however that might be expressed.

One might ask why neither Moses nor Jesus spoke concerning acceptable reasons for divorce. Jesus understood, as well as Moses, that attempting to establish acceptable or non-acceptable reasons for divorce through civil law could not begin to adequately address the issue. It would be like grasping after shadows. If a man has a hardened heart against his wife, civil law cannot change this or hold him accountable. Civil law can only attempt to penalize specific hostile outward expressions of the hardened heart like murder, adultery, physical abuse, or desertion. Civil law cannot control the myriad of subtle and yet destructive expressions of the hardened heart.

If a man has a hardened heart, stubbornly refusing to repent from his evil ways, he can make life "hell on earth" for his spouse without breaking a single civil law. God does not intend for people to continue to live under such abuse. Jesus came to set captives free, not to enslave people in oppressive (much less abusive) relationships. Moses, speaking under divine inspiration, recognized that people harden their hearts and thus marriages break up. In an effort to stop the further oppression of women, he legislatively endorsed the bill of divorce. In doing so, he did not establish specific acceptable reasons or procedures for divorce, but allowed these to be worked out domestically, and to a small degree influenced or controlled by local civil government.

Not only is legislation not the answer, but mankind is not wise enough to administer any such legislation. We cannot clearly discern the motives of our own hearts, much less the motives of someone else! *"The human heart is most deceitful and desperately wicked. Who really knows how bad it is?"* (Jeremiah 17:9 NLT) All outward indications might point to a husband being the one at fault because his wife has maligned him for leaving the family; when in truth, the wife may regularly push his buttons, manipulating him in order to make him look bad and her look like a "suffering saint." Hypocrisy is treacherous.

Consider the wife who has found companionship and comfort in the arms of a man other than her husband. For years her husband has secretly emotionally and psychologically abused her. Satan brings another man into her life and she falls into adultery. In her heart though, she is broken, contrite, and truly repentant. She tries to break off the relationship, knowing that it is wrong, but is emotionally addicted to it like heroin. On the other hand, her husband is hard-hearted, unforgiving, and constantly throws her sin in her face, and completely rejects her efforts at reconciliation. She is ultimately branded an adulteress and ostracized by her church, friends and possibly even her family; but the husband is publicly vindicated for divorcing her.

What judge, other than God Himself, is able to discern the motives of the heart, much less unravel the tangled web of a human relationship? Establishing acceptable and non-acceptable reasons for divorce is not the answer to divorce. Only true repentance, a change of heart, can keep death from working in relationships, especially marriages!

God desires us to honor and love one another—especially our spouses.

He desires for us to be tenderhearted and gentle with each other; and God hopes that we will always honor and uphold our marriage covenants. But in His infinite wisdom, He allows us freedom of choice, even to sin. If a person chooses to harden his heart against his spouse, God allows divorce as a means of cutting the marital bond in order to prevent greater sorrow and as a means of holding one accountable for his actions. Law exists in order to hinder us from hurting each other and ourselves—not to *cause* us pain, but to keep us *from* pain.

When we sin against God and our spouses, we open the door for Satan to wreak havoc in our lives and the lives of our loved ones. God personally wrote the Ten Commandments in stone, one of which is, *"You shall not commit adultery"* (Exodus 20:14 NKJV). Adultery is much more than just a sexual sin; it is a sin of the heart against your spouse and marriage union. People who continue to sin against their spouses, stubbornly refusing to repent, to change the way they think, speak, and act towards their spouses, will eventually bring death to their marital relationships. Marriage is valuable and breakable and should be treated as such.

Embracing the truth that God is intimately involved in marriage and having a healthy reverential respect of God should motivate us to do everything we can to honor our marriage relationships! Thankfully though, God allows divorce for people caught in destructive relationships to avert greater suffering and pain, and to give them hope for a better tomorrow.

Jesus is the champion of freedom for all people. His primary thrust in ministry is to bring personal spiritual freedom from sin to the inner person; but many things He said and did have resulted in social freedom for the oppressed, especially for women, children, and slaves. This is a dynamic reality here in United States of America where a single truth embraced in our Constitution— that all people are created equal—has brought about increasing political, social, and economic freedom for all races and both genders. Total equality has not been attained, but we, as a nation, are much better off than we were one hundred or even twenty years ago. True personal spiritual freedom brings about increasing relational, physical, mental, emotional, and financial freedom for all who embrace Jesus–the embodiment of truth.

By the power of the Holy Spirit, Jesus' teaching on the divine ideal of marriage and the true cause of divorce, the hardness of heart, a stubborn refusal to repent, brought tremendous conviction to those present. We can be confident that those present heard the passion in His voice concerning this issue and felt His increasing frustration and anger concerning the Pharisees and their legalistic and licentious mindset.

Most people greatly desire and need the love, companionship, and healthy sexual fulfillment that can only be found in marriage. Laws concerning acceptable reasons for divorce or punishment of divorcées are not the answer to the plague of divorce. The answer can only be found in freedom from sin and deliverance from a hardened heart. These are found in Christ through repentance–a change in our hearts!

Divorce is never easy, nor without serious negative ramifications, but divorce is not sin, in and of itself, any more than death is. Divorce is a type of death being the separation of two people who have been yoked together as one interdependent family unit. Divorce can be sin if it is the action of a hardened heart. However, divorce can also be the best thing to do in a bad situation if motivated out of the love of God.

God, in His perfect love for Israel, divorced her (Jeremiah 3:8) because she needed to be held accountable for her stubborn refusal to repent. She needed to be separated from God's love and protection in the hope that she might turn from her evil ways back to God. There are situations where the most loving thing a woman can do for her husband is to divorce him, holding him accountable for his sins against her, their children, and God. To God's credit and praise, after saying that He divorced Israel, He also promised to take her back if she would only abandon her adulterous lovers and return to Him wholeheartedly!

A contextually based understanding of Jesus' comments on divorce in no way supports the traditional doctrine of divorce! Jesus did not condemn divorcées. He did not contradict or disagree with the Law of Moses, nor did Jesus intend to give "teeth to the law," making it more strict. He did not say or imply that a divorced person should remain celibate.

However, Jesus did elevate women by holding men accountable for the way they treat their wives. He revealed marriage as a work of God, something that God has a vital interest in. Jesus revealed that adultery is more than just a sexual sin; it is a sin of the heart against one's spouse. One can also logically deduce that Jesus recognized and endorsed the need for civil regulation of marriage, divorce, and remarriage. Jesus affirmed the divine ideal of marriage, and yet realistically endorsed divorce as a proper end to a broken relationship and as a means of holding each other accountable in love.

# Chapter XIX
# PAUL'S FATHERLY COUNSEL

In the first century, the city of Corinth had an estimated 650,000 people, including approximately 400,000 slaves, being second only to Rome in population. It was an international city with citizens from all over the then known civilized world. It was a wealthy city, being a major center of trade for the entire Mediterranean area. Products from Rome, Egypt, Spain, Israel, Phoenicia and Asia Minor flowed like a river through its ports.

Most large cities and even smaller ones today have a relatively well-known street or district where people can arrange to satisfy their most immoral desires, like Amsterdam's "red-light district." Some cities have a reputation for being wholly given over to a certain vise. Corinth was one such city—full of open, unrestrained sexual immorality. Throughout the Roman world, Corinth was known as a city of unbridled lust and perversion. In fact, the Greek word "to corinthianize" means to live shamelessly and immorally.

Corinth had at least twelve different temples—the most famous of which was built to honor Aphrodite, the goddess of love. Temple prostitution was a means of worship for the parishioners and a means of financial income for the temple. More than one thousand prostitutes worked in "honor" of Aphrodite and serviced the sexual lust of the people within the city.

In the middle of this perversion, the Apostle Paul planted a church. Paul worked in Corinth for approximately eighteen months and, by the grace of God, the church in Corinth became one of the larger of the first century. A few years after leaving Corinth, Paul received word of serious problems in the church, which provided the impetus for the writing of I Corinthians.

In I Corinthians, Paul deals with a wide range of topics: division in the church; a case of incest; civil lawsuits between Christians; chaos in worship services; immorality; marital problems; pagan festivals; abuse of spiritual gifts; and doctrinal error concerning the resurrection of the dead. If the book of Romans is a systematic theological treatise, I Corinthians is an impassioned plea from a father to his children to repent of their immoral lifestyles and to live righteously. Paul uses logical arguments, emotional pleas, sarcasm, poetry, and personal testimony to move the church to repentance. This passionate Apostle gives his best counsel to help the church overcome these troubling issues. In chapter seven, in the middle of this fiery letter, Paul briefly touches on a few specific marital issues.

In the first verse of chapter seven, Paul says that he will answer questions that he was asked in a letter that he received from the church in Corinth. The Contemporary English Version highlights the first question.

I Corinthians 7:1 (CEV)
*Now I will answer the questions that you asked in your letter.
You asked, "Is it best for people not to marry?"*

Other translations do not recognize the second part of this verse as a question. Rather it is translated as a declaration, *"It is good not to marry"* (NIV). Understood as a question, the passage fits better its immediate literary context. Before we look at Paul's response, let us postulate a few possible reasons why marriage would be a point of contention in the Church at Corinth.

One of the first things that Paul deals with in his letter to the Corinthians is a sectarian attitude in the church. Some claimed to follow Paul, others followed Apollos, Peter, or Christ (I Corinthians 1:12). People who claimed to follow Paul probably meant that they wished to emulate Paul, his lifestyle, and ministry above others—not that Paul taught anything different than Peter, Apollos, or Christ. Paul was their hero, their celebrity idol, someone they wished to pattern their lives after in every way. They considered his devotion to God above anyone they had met. Celebrity worship can be a powerful motivation.

It could be that some people idolized Paul so much that they desired to remain or become single like Paul and even arrogantly promoted celibacy as the most righteous and holy way to live for Christ. They could have considered married couples to be, at best, second-rate citizens of the Kingdom of God. As discussed previously, this came to be a predominant attitude in the early Roman church.

Not only was Paul single and celibate, but so was Christ. What devotion! What self-sacrifice! What a man of God! Surely, God thinks more highly of people who are celibate for His name's sake, than of people who are married and indulge the lust of their flesh! (Of course I'm speaking sarcastically.) People could have idolized Paul so much that, if they were married, they even considered divorce or at least abstaining from sexual intimacy though remaining married.

It is also possible, as speculated by some Christian scholars, that Paul himself was a divorcé and chose to remain single in order to serve Christ without distraction. Paul implies in I Corinthians 9:5 that he was not married at the time, choosing not to take a wife with him on his missionary journeys. However, before becoming a Christian, Paul was a Pharisee and a member of the Jewish counsel in Jerusalem.

A good Pharisee would have been married in order to fulfill the command to procreate; and it is unlikely that a single man would have been chosen to be a member of the Jewish counsel in Jerusalem, much less a respected member and student of Rabbi Gamaliel. The Talmud states, *"He who has no wife is not a proper man"* (bYeb.63). Paul speaks of himself as a *"Hebrew of Hebrews; concerning the Law, a Pharisee"* (Philippians 3:5 NKJV). Though not conclusive, this is substantial evidence supporting the belief that Paul was married before his conversion to Christianity. If Paul was married at that time, it is possible that his wife chose not to follow him after he became a Christian. A Jewish wife would have had morally acceptable and even socially commendable grounds to seek a divorce from a husband who had joined the persecuted Christian sect.

Those who wished to emulate Paul would consider doing the same, leaving their unbelieving wives in order to devote their full passion and energy to Christian service. Being a divorcé would also explain Paul's understanding and compassion for those in a similar situation. Of course, Paul being a divorcé is just speculation; he could have been a widower, although one would think that if his wife had died, she would have been mentioned somewhere in his writings. Whereas, divorce is not something people are proud of.

Another problem possibly faced by some people in the church at Corinth would have been a radical reaction to the perverse sexual lifestyle prevalent in their city. People who have been delivered from significant bondage to a specific sin often go to the opposite extreme and hate that sin and anything or anyone tainted by it. For example, people who have quit smoking often cannot stand to be around people who smoke. The slightest hint of smoke in the air totally repulses them. Ex-drug addicts often become strong supporters of the war on drugs. Homosexuals who are freed from such perversion often found or support ministries working to deliver others caught up in this deviant and destructive lifestyle. Considering this human tendency, it would be understandable if people who were given over to the sexual immorality common in Corinth, once having given their lives to Christ, developing a radical abhorrence of sexual intercourse, even within their marriages.

As was mentioned previously, Platonic and Stoic philosophy would have also significantly influenced the people of Corinth. Freeing one's self from passion was a goal of the Stoics; and Platonic philosophy encouraged the use of the will to exalt the intellect and suppress the passions.

Like a loving father correcting his errant children, in I Corinthians 7, Paul briefly addresses a problem in the Church of Corinth, the issue of singleness as a preferred lifestyle in serving the Lord. Paul begins by affirming that being married is advantageous in that it can keep one from sexual immorality (v. 2). Because of this, a husband and wife should not refuse to be intimate with each other; rather, they should seek to fulfill each other's needs and desires (v. 3-5).

Paul then mentions that he wishes everyone could be single like him, but he realizes that people have different needs, desires, and aptitudes (v. 7); and he specifically said that his desire for people to remain single is not a command from God, but something he said by permission (v. 6). So, if you are single and can contain yourself, don't seek to get married (v. 8); but if you burn with passion, please do get married (v. 9); and if you are already married, don't get a divorce! Why? Because Jesus clearly taught that a married person should not leave his/her spouse (v. 10-11).

As previously discussed, Jesus clearly affirmed the divine ideal that marriage was to be a life-long monogamous, faithful union between a man and woman. He noted that divorce was allowed because of the hardness of heart in mankind, and instituted to stop the satanic practice of a man abandoning his wife, making her an adulteress.

Why does Paul mention Jesus' teaching on marriage? Recall that Paul is answering the question, or possibly refuting the assertion that "It is best for people not to marry." He recognized that some of the congregation idolized him. Paul thus mentions Jesus' teaching on marriage in order to encourage married couples to remain faithful to each other and not think that they could serve God better if they divorced their spouses and lived celibate the remainder of their lives.

We need to keep in mind that Paul is addressing a specific problem in the church. In doing so, he applies overarching principles in giving advice concerning that problem. He is not establishing new principles or precepts, nor is he giving a thorough doctrinal instruction on marriage, divorce, and remarriage. His statements should be understood in the context of the question that he is answering. To interpret them to say more than what the literary context dictates can quickly lead to doctrinal error.

Paul then gives his informed, authoritative, and possibly experientially based advice concerning the issue of mixed marriages between Christians and non-Christians (7:12-17). Apparently, some Christians in this situation believed that it would be better if they left their unbelieving spouses, even if their spouses wished to remain married to them. In support of their belief, they could have cited the case in Ezra 10:3 where God commanded the Israelites to divorce their pagan spouses. If it is true that Paul was a divorcé, they could have also referenced him as an example to support leaving an unbelieving spouse. In order to correct this errant belief, Paul instructs that if the nonbeliever wishes to remain in the marriage, the believer should remain faithful (7:12-13). He then gives the reason behind this instruction. As long as the nonbeliever is married to the Christian, the non-believer is sanctified—set apart for a special work of the Spirit of God in his heart and life. Remaining married to the unbeliever also releases a tremendously powerful Godly influence in the lives of their children (7:14), especially as opposed to the terrible seeds of destruction that would be sown through a divorce in such cases.

If the unbeliever is adamant about getting a divorce, Paul instructs that the Christian should allow it and that the Christian is *"not under bondage in such cases"* (I Corinthians 7:15 KJV). This is commonly called the "Pauline Privilege." Many ministers that hold to a modified traditional doctrine of divorce believe that Paul was establishing another "acceptable" reason for divorce other than adultery; but as was previously established, neither Jesus, nor Moses established "acceptable" or "non-acceptable" reasons for divorce. God graciously and compassionately allows divorce because one or both spouses harden their hearts against each other. The fruit of the hardened heart could be adultery, abandonment, alcoholism, emotional or physical abuse, or even something as subjective as irreconcilable differences.

Those who hold tightly to the traditional doctrine of divorce would read into this passage that Paul is only referring to separation and not divorce. In the cultural context of that day, this is a ludicrous assertion. To leave your spouse, meant to divorce your spouse. In the Greco-Roman cultural context there was not even a need for a bill of divorce to enact the divorce, simply leaving accomplished that for either party.

Rather than Paul legislatively adding an "acceptable" reason for divorce, Paul is simply giving wise counsel concerning the situation at hand and pointing out the fundamental principles that his children in the faith need to wrestle with in making their own personal decisions. The principles he mentions are the divine ideal of marriage and God's call on our lives to live in peace. In this case, Paul advises that if the non-believer is adamant about leaving, the believer should let the unbeliever go with divorce being assumed by their cultural context (7:15).

The principle of the divine ideal of marriage should motivate believers to do everything possible to keep their marriages together and be a blessing to their spouses. The principle of living in peace with your fellow man moves believers to do whatever is within their power to live peaceful lives. In some situations, in order to live in peace, the believer must quit fighting and let their unbelieving spouse leave–divorce.

In I Corinthians 7:15, Paul reassures believers that in such cases they are *"not under bondage"* (KJV). "Bondage" comes from the Greek word δέω **děō**, *deh'-o* that means "to bind." Derivatives of this word are also used in v. 27, *"Art thou bound unto a wife? Seek not to be loosed"* (KJV); and in v. 39, *"The wife is bound by the law as long as her husband liveth"* (KJV). Both of these verses refer to marriage, but in verse 15, Paul is NOT technically defining how or when the marital bond is broken. He is making a generalized statement recognizing the breaking of the marital bond (divorce), and freeing the believer of any sense of obligation before the Lord to strive further to keep the marriage together.

Please keep in mind that I Corinthians 7 is not a complete theological treatise on marriage, divorce and remarriage. Paul is answering specific questions, dealing with any related incorrect beliefs or attitudes that he perceives, reinforcing broad principles by which Christians are to live by, and briefly explaining how he came to his conclusions and advice.

Another provocative verse in this passage clearly says that <u>if a divorcé marries, he does not sin</u>! This is the exact opposite of what the traditional doctrine of divorce teaches. It would say that divorcées are not to marry again; if they do marry again, they sin. Some people go so far as to say that if divorcées marry again, they not only sin, but God does not recognize their marriages; therefore, they are living in adultery.

I Corinthians 7:27 says, *"Art thou bound unto a wife? Seek not to be loosed. Art thou loosed from a wife? Seek not a wife"* (KJV). *"Loosed"* in this passage refers to a breaking of the marital bond. *"Loosed"* is set in contrast to *"bound,"* clearly reinforcing the concept that *"loosed"* equates divorce. *"Loosed"* is a derivative of λύω **luō**, *loo'-o* which means to loosen, break up, destroy, or dissolve. Paul in essence says, *"If you are married, do not seek a divorce. If you are divorced, do not seek to get married again."* If the passage stopped there, it would appear to endorse the traditional doctrine, BUT the next verse says, *"But and if thou marry, **thou hast not sinned**"* (I Corinthians 7:28a

KJV). The Holy Bible from Ancient Eastern Manuscripts actually translates this passage as, *"If you are divorced from a wife, do not seek a wife. But if you marry, you do not sin"* (I Corinthians 7:27b -28a).

The immediate literary context of this verse demands this interpretation. Proponents of the traditional doctrine assert that in this passage, Paul only references separation but not divorce. If this is true then Paul is endorsing polygamy because if this passage is about separation, then the man that is separated from his wife does not sin if he marries another woman, which is polygamy. Consequently, the simplest interpretation is also the best, *"If you are divorced, do not seek to marry, but if you do, you do not sin!"*

Furthermore, notice in this statement that Paul does not qualify what categories of divorcées may or may not marry. Because of the tremendous immorality of the city and the size of the Corinthian church, there would likely have been a large variety of divorcées. This could have included those who at the time of their divorce were Christians and those who were non-Christians; those who had been divorced several times and those who had only been married once, those who divorced their spouses for morally acceptable reasons and those who divorced their spouses for selfish, hateful reasons. Note that Paul makes no distinction between these categories or their ability to remarry.

We must also remember that Paul's advice for the divorcé not to remarry is the same advice that he gave all single people—divorcées, virgins, and widows. I use the word "advice" rather than "direction" or "command" because Paul made it clear at the beginning of Chapter 7 that he is not setting forth a new doctrine of celibacy. He simply encourages all singles (virgins, widows, and divorcées) to consider remaining unmarried so that they may be free of many of this world's concerns and devote their lives to the Lord.

If you are divorced and you marry again you do not sin! What a contradiction to the traditional doctrine of divorce! Sadly, most modern translations evade this issue by mistranslating the passage. Rather than translating the second "loosed" as "divorced," it is translated as "unmarried" even though "unmarried" does not fit the literary context and must be read into the passage—bad exegesis.

The Apostle Paul in I Corinthians 7 does not support the traditional doctrine of divorce! He does recognize and support the divine ideal of marriage and encourages all singles to consider remaining single because of the trials of the day, the freedom from certain cares of the world, and the ability to devote one's complete life to the things of the Lord. Paul also recognizes that not all people are gifted in this way; and that if people burn with sexual desire, they should get married; and Paul specifically says that divorcées do not sin if they marry again!

Another controversial passage by Paul concerns guidelines for church leadership. Paul says in I Timothy 3:1-2a, *"This is a faithful saying: If a man desires the position of a bishop, he desires a good work. A bishop then must be blameless, the husband of one wife"* (NKJV). The phrase, *"husband of one wife,"* is interpreted as *"married only once"* (NRSV & NAB), implying a divorcé may not be a bishop; *"must have only one wife"* (NCV), implying that Paul was forbidding polygamy; *"faithful to his wife"* (NLT), and *"faithful in marriage"* (NCV), implying the need for faithfulness in covenant relationships, especially in marriage.

What does *"husband of one wife"* mean? Does it forbid divorcés from being leaders in the church? What about widowers who have remarried? Is it meant to be a stance against polygamy? Does it mean that one must be married to be a leader, thus excluding singles? Could it simply mean a faithful person, especially in marriage if one is married? What was the authorial intent?

Another similar phrase in I Timothy, *"the wife of one man"* (1 Tim. 5:9 NKJV), eliminates some of the possible interpretations. In this passage, Paul gives guidelines as to the widows who may be added to the list of women who were to receive ongoing support from the church. In subsequent verses, Paul instructs younger widows to marry and thus not be a burden to the church, or become gossips and busybodies.

The phrase *"wife of one man"* eliminates the possibility that Paul is speaking about polygamy, because polyandry, women with multiple husbands, was unheard of in New Testament times, in Ancient Near Eastern Jewish, Greek, and Roman cultures. It is also unlikely that *"wife of one man"* refers to widows who have remarried. Paul instructs younger widows to remarry, and it is unthinkable that a widow who remarried according to Paul's instructions would later be denied care from the church if she was widowed a second time when she was older and unable to remarry. Thus it is unlikely that *"husband of one wife"* refers to either a prohibition against polygamy or a widower who has remarried becoming a leader in the church.

It is also extremely unlikely that *"husband of one wife"* means that a leader in the church must be married and cannot be single. This concept is not consistent with Paul's statements in 1 Corinthians 7 that singles should remain unmarried so as better to serve the Lord. Why would Paul in one place say that it is better to remain single so that one may fully serve the Lord, and in another place say that if one desires to be in leadership, one must be married? Paul himself was not married, so it does not make sense that he would require other leaders in the church to be married. Requiring leadership to be married would also contradict Jesus' statement that some people stay single for the sake of the Kingdom of God (Matthew 19:12). Doctrine should be built upon the preponderance of applicable scripture, not individual statements, especially those that are not explicit. It is thus highly improbable that *"husband of one wife"* is intended to legislate the marital status of church leadership.

Concerning divorcés, it also unlikely that *"husband of one wife"* is a prohibition of such becoming leaders in the church. This interpretation's foundation is the errant belief that marriage is indissoluble. If marriage were indissoluble, then a divorced man would actually still be married to his first wife, though living in an adulterous marriage with another woman. However, divorce, just like death, breaks the marriage bond. Thus a divorcé who has remarried is the husband of only one woman and is not living in adultery, just like a widower who has remarried.

If Paul intended to forbid divorcés (single or remarried) from being in leadership, he would have most certainly not used such an ambiguous term as *"husband of one wife."* Furthermore, the interpretation, *"not a divorcé"* does not fit the tone of the passage or the Gospel of the New Testament. Paul writes concerning current character qualities, not past sins or former evil lifestyles. A man could have been a drunk in the past, but is now sober. He could have lived a homosexual lifestyle. He could have been a fornicator, living with many women though having never married. He could have been a violent and murderous man who persecuted the church, like Paul. But having come to Christ, he was forgiven of such sins and started a new life. The concept that divorcés are forbidden from being leaders in the church is against the Gospel message of forgiveness and new life for the believer. It is thus very unlikely that *"husband of one wife"* is in any way a reference to divorce.

*"Husband of one wife"* is thus best interpreted as *"faithful in marriage,"* or *"being a person of high sexual morality."* David Instone-Brewer notes that:

> The Early Church could not escape the effect of the surrounding culture. The epistles show that even among Christians, loose sexual morals were not unknown. The frequent exhortations about sexual morality suggest that this was a pressing concern in the Early Church and a practical problem for many individuals. Jesus had very little to say about sexual misconduct, other than immorality committed "in the heart," because the vast proportion of Jewish society already had very high sexual morals. Yet believers from a non-Jewish background came from a very different culture, and it is clear that they sometimes found it difficult to leave behind their Greco-Roman lifestyle.
>
> In this context it was necessary to make sure that the leaders of the Church were people who were known to be faithful to their partners. It was not enough that they were technically faithful—in the Greco-Roman world one could have a mistress without being guilty of adultery—they had to be known as someone who "has eyes for only one woman" (as we would say in modern English), that is, as a "husband of one wife."[39]

A *"one woman kind of man,"* a man who is faithful in his relationships, especially in regards to his marriage, this is the kind of leader a church needs. A bishop should be a person who has a track record of being mature and faithful in his relationships, a man of holiness and sexual purity in thought and deed. If he is married, he should be faithful, having eyes only for his wife!

# *Chapter XX*
# WHAT IF

## DOESN'T GOD HATE DIVORCE?

A scripture often quoted in discussions about divorce is Malachi 2:16; *"For the LORD, the God of Israel, saith that he hateth putting away: for one covereth violence with his garment, saith the LORD of hosts: therefore take heed to your spirit, that ye deal not treacherously"* (KJV). (emphasis mine) Most modern English versions translate the highlighted words as God saying, **"I hate divorce."** Usually, the person quoting this passage interprets it as a blanket statement of condemnation against all divorce. It is also often used as a proof text that divorce, in and of itself, is sin. Is this correct?

One of the main themes of the book of Malachi is a call to covenant faithfulness, particularly in our relationship with God. Malachi 2:10-16 presents a progressively specific list of examples where the Israelites were being unfaithful in their covenant relationships. In 2:10 they are chastised in general for being unfaithful to their covenants with each other. In 2:11-12 they are specifically denounced for breaking their covenant with God by marrying non-Jewish women. The series culminates in 2:13-16 with the proclamation that God does not hear their prayers or accept their sacrificial offerings because they have broken their marriage covenants. There is sufficient literary context to suggest that these men were actually leaving their now older "wives of their youth" in order to marry the younger, more exotic, and possibly richer foreign women.

Notice that the word "he" in the aforementioned quote of verse 2:16

in the King James Version is not capitalized. As noted before, the King James Version is a wooden, literal version that attempts to stick closely to a word for word translation of the original language. The word "he" is not capitalized because in the Hebrew, it is unclear whether the "he" in "he hates putting away" refers to God or is a reference to someone or something else. In fact, a few phrases in verses 2:14-16 are difficult to translate as evident by the way they are translated in the King James Version. Note the differences between the following translations of this passage.

King James Version
*Yet ye say, Wherefore? Because the LORD hath been witness between thee and the wife of thy youth, against whom thou hast dealt treacherously: yet is she thy companion, and the wife of thy covenant.* **And did not he make one? Yet had he the residue of the spirit. And wherefore one? That he might seek a godly seed.** *Therefore take heed to your spirit, and let none deal treacherously against the wife of his youth.* **For the LORD, the God of Israel, saith that** *he hateth putting away: for one covereth violence with his garment, saith the LORD of hosts: therefore take heed to your spirit, that ye deal not treacherously.* (emphasis mine)

Hugenberger
*You ask, "Why does he not?" Because the LORD was witness between you and the wife of your youth, against whom you have been faithless, though she is your companion and your wife by covenant.* **Did He not make [you/them] one, with a remnant of the spirit belonging to it? And what was the One seeking? A godly seed!** *Therefore watch out for your lives and do not act faithlessly against the wife of your youth.* **If** <u>**one hates and divorces**</u> **[that is, if one divorces merely on the grounds of aversion], says Yahweh, God of Israel, he covers his garments with violence [i.e., such a man visibly defiles himself with violence]**, *says Yahweh of hosts. Therefore, take heed to yourselves and do not be faithless [against your wife]."* (emphasis mine)[40]

Note the difficulty that is evident in the translation of verse 15. Modern translations vary dramatically on this passage. Hugenberger's translation is compelling though, especially the connection one may draw between "A godly seed!" and Jesus, the promised seed of the woman in Genesis 3:15 that would destroy Satan. It was because of God's plan to bring redemption through Jesus, that God was so serious about the Israelites not intermarrying with the surrounding nations.

Concerning verse 16, recall that in our previous discussion of Deuteronomy 24:1-4, was mentioned the "hateful divorce." David Instone-Brewer notes concerning verse 16:

> The Hebrew reads "he hates divorce" which most translations emend to "I hate divorce." Hugenberger relies on Raymond Westbrook,[41] who pointed out the parallel with ancient Near Eastern texts, which use the phrase "He hates (and) divorce." He showed that this phrase meant "he divorces without adequate grounds." This was a legal distinction between a divorce which was based on grounds such as adultery or neglect (which resulted in financial penalty for the guilty partner) and a divorce where no grounds could be cited (which resulted in a financial penalty for the person bringing the divorce).
>
> Either way, verse 16 shows that God is against the person who break's one's marriage vows. The more traditional interpretations may seem to suggest that God is against divorce of any kind, but the context clearly shows that this is not so. The constantly reiterated theme of these verses is faithfulness to the terms of the marriage covenant. Criticism is not directed at the person who carries out the divorce, but the person who causes the divorce by not being faithful to the marriage covenant.[42]

It is evident that the "hateful divorce" interpretation fits the context of the verse, the book, the Old Testament, and the culture of the Middle East, much better than the "'I hate divorce,' says God" interpretation. Malachi 2:10-16 also reveals the passion of God against unfaithfulness. The word, בָּגַד , **bâgad**, *baw-gad'*, which means to be treacherously unfaithful is repeated five times. Any teacher or public speaker knows that repetition is a powerful means of reinforcing an idea or concept.

In the Old Testament **bâgad** is used primarily to describe a person or a people that does not honor and consistently breaks treaties, covenants, or contracts. It is used to describe Judah in Jeremiah 3:7, 8, & 10 (the passage from which I base the title of this book). If God hated divorce, surely He would not have used divorce as a metaphor in Jeremiah 3:8 of His rejection of Israel for their unfaithfulness to their covenant with Him, nor would He have commanded the Israelites to divorce their foreign wives, as He did in Ezra 10:3. God does not hate divorce; however, He does hate treacherous unfaithfulness as often expressed in divorce!

## What If The Church Allows Divorce?

This question **"assumes"** that the church has the authority to either allow or forbid divorce. However, the church does NOT have such authority. Issues concerning marriage and divorce are under *civil* authority. Does this mean that the church has no influence concerning marriage and divorce? Obviously not! The church has tremendous authority and responsibility to speak into the lives of individuals, communities, and nations. We are the salt and the light of this world. Our job is to retard decay, inspire a thirst for Jesus, and bring illumination.

Our primary influence is through prayer, destroying the principalities and powers of darkness that are influencing people, cities, and nations. The church, individually and corporately, should also be involved in civil government, influencing the establishment and enforcement of civil law that is inspired by biblical principles, law, and morality. If we wish to positively influence any situation, we must do so with the proper authority and through the correct authority structures.

*No Authority equals No Power!* Without the authority to legislate or the power to enforce their wishes, people turn to coercion and manipulation in order to control others. Let us rise above this tendency and focus our efforts on strengthening and empowering individuals and couples, not trying to control them through falsely assumed religious authority!

## WHAT IF THE STATE ALLOWS HOMOSEXUAL MARRIAGES?

Another question often raised is, "If the civil government has the authority to declare the viability of marriages, then should we, the church, recognize and allow homosexual marriages if (may God forbid) our civil government does so?" This might sound shocking, but the church has no authority to declare that a homosexual couple is or is not married. If civil law allows it, they are married–a legal and social covenant has been established, though it is an *unholy* covenant.

The church may admit that the homosexual couple is married; but the Bible clearly teaches that homosexual relationships and lifestyles are a perversion of nature and an abomination to God. *Therefore, if a "married" homosexual came to Christ or desired to join a local church, he would need to get a divorce and stop practicing the sin of homosexuality.* In like manner, a thief or murderer who comes to Christ needs to stop the sins of stealing or murdering, and an adulterer should stop committing adultery. The same principles apply to a heterosexual couple that is living together like husband and wife without being married—fornication. They would need to either get married or stop living together.

A similar biblical example of people marrying who were commanded by God not to marry is the Israelites intermarrying with surrounding nations. During a revival of the rule of God in their hearts and in their nation, God through Ezra the priest instructed them to divorce their Gentile wives (Ezra 10:10, 11). The Bible does not specifically forbid homosexual marriages, but it does forbid any type of homosexual relationships. *Therefore if the civil government condones homosexual marriages, the church should exclude from communion and fellowship anyone who continues in such a relationship, married or otherwise.*

## WHAT IF THE CHURCH RECOGNIZES THAT MARRIAGE IS DISSOLUBLE?

People have expressed the concern that, "If people think that marriage is breakable and divorce is an option, will that not lead to an increase in divorce?" It's been said that an unguarded strength is a double weakness. If people believe that marriage is indissoluble, they might tend to neglect it, leaving it unguarded and open to attack. However, if people recognize that marriage is breakable and divorce is a possibility, they should be motivated to treat their spouses with more respect and love. Husbands and wives need to realize that if they consistently do not honor their marital commitments and do not treat their spouses as they should, their marriages may eventually end in divorce.

Grace and forgiveness, versus judgement and law, have always been at conflict in the heart of man, and are truths that are held in dynamic tension in the Word of God. When the Apostle Paul taught on the unequivocal grace of God, some asked if grace gives us a license to sin (Romans 6:15). In no way does grace empower us to sin! Grace, the undeserved favor of God, actually frees us from sin. The truth regarding marriage being breakable will do the same thing; it will free people to stop sinning against each other and against God.

Few, if any, couples marry with the expectation of divorce. Most couples marry because they desire to establish a life-long relationship of committed love. Sadly, due to our selfish nature, we can harden our hearts against our spouses and destroy the very homes that we established to bring us love, joy, and peace. *Divorce, in and of itself, is not sin, but it is always the result of sin!*

Marriage was given to mankind to be a blessing, not a curse—to be a little heaven on earth, not hell on earth! Like the Sabbath, marriage was made for man, not man for marriage. On the other hand, the traditional doctrine of divorce would bind a person in an abusive relationship rather than hold the abuser accountable! Equipping people to establish godly personal boundaries in all relationships, especially in marriage, should be part of the ministry of every local church.

## WILL THIS HELP A PERSON "JUSTIFY" HIS/HER DIVORCE?

Some have expressed their concern that people either contemplating divorce or having divorced their spouses will use the teachings of this book to "justify" their divorces. Frankly, it is my hope that this book will free some people to do just that–justify their divorces. For the woman whose husband is abusing her or her children, I pray that this book empowers her to not only divorce her husband with the full support of the church if he refuses to repent, but to even throw him in jail if needed!

For the husband whose wife is running around on him and refuses to change her ways, I hope that this book empowers him to "pray through" and discern God's will. He must decide to either divorce her with the full conviction that he's doing the best and most loving thing in a bad situation, or to hang-in-there with the full assurance of faith that God is going to turn it around, and protect them both from sexually transmitted diseases. For divorcées who are wrapped in the lies of the traditional doctrine, believing that they can never marry again, I pray that this book will free them to seek God for marriages that will bring them great happiness.

On the other hand, in no way do I wish to empower people to justify their divorces if they are based on selfish reasons! It is my earnest prayer that through the truth contained in this book, and the anointing of the Holy Spirit that I pray is upon this book, that they will turn from such selfishness and allow God to heal their marriages or repent of the hardness of heart that led to their divorces.

To justify means "to prove or show to be just, right, or reasonable; to show to have had a sufficient legal reason."[43] People considering divorce need to "justify" it with God, family, friends, and within their own hearts and minds. One brother, during the process of justifying before God, divorcing his wife, understood the Lord to say to him that God would bless him if he divorced his wife. But, if he hung-in-there and waited on God to work things out, God would tremendously bless him! He chose to wait on God, and God not only restored his marriage making it much better than it was before her infidelity, but God also blessed him wonderfully in many other areas of his life, especially in his ministry. On the other hand, others might hear the Lord release them from abusive and destructive relationships.

"To justify" implies judgement. Ultimately, a woman's decision to divorce her husband is between herself, her husband, the state, and God. These are the proper authorities over that marriage. Other people, even their children, have no authority or responsibility to set in judgement and declare the righteousness or unrighteousness of such divorces, much less to impose any type of punishment. In the final analysis, only God and the couple know what goes on behind closed doors. When tempted to or even asked to declare a divorce right or wrong, we need to be like Jesus and ask *"Friend, who made me a judge over you to decide such things as that?"* (Luke 12:14 NLT).

## WHAT ABOUT MARRIAGES THAT ARE HAVING PROBLEMS?

A good friend and brother in Christ asked me how my stated beliefs on divorce would apply to him and his wife. Several years ago he committed adultery and continues to have a terrible struggle with lust to this day. From what he said, he and his wife are still married today primarily because they believe it would be a grievous and almost unforgivable sin for them to get a divorce. Before, and especially since he committed adultery, they have struggled in many areas of their relationship—especially with sexual and emotional intimacy. Both desire to work things out and provide a happy home for their children, but there are constant struggles between them. The husband burns with sexual passion, but his wife refuses to be sexually intimate with him. The wife yearns for emotional security and love, but her husband has not been able to overcome the pain he has caused her and rebuild the trust in their relationship that he destroyed through his infidelity.

The first thing that they both need to realize is that their marriage is not indissoluble or unbreakable; in fact, without help their marriage might completely dissolve. They are already divided emotionally and sexually; and they have started distancing themselves from each other psychologically, consistently thinking evil of each other.

If they wish their marriage to survive, even flourish, they need to focus on meeting their partners' needs, especially in the two weakest dimensions of their marriage—intimacy physically and emotionally. While being mindful not to allow the other dimensions to rip further apart, they need to purposefully allocate available resources of time, energy, and money toward mending the rifts in their relationship—emotionally and sexually. Both need to recognize that the condition of their hearts—hard or soft—will eventually determine the outcome of their marriage. Thankfully, they both have a passionate love for the Lord and for their children. These two dimensions alone have the power to keep the marriage together long enough for healing to take place in the other dimensions.

Married couples that are not having serious problems also need to recognize that their marriages are fragile. This should motivate us to build hedges of protection around our marriages. These hedges of protection should include installed regular maintenance programs, special continuing education units, and regular checkups.

Several years ago, Chantal and I attended a Marriage Encounter weekend, a special "continuing education unit." Marriage Encounter weekends are provided by several different denominations, but all use the same basic format. It turned out to be a significant positive turning point in our marriage. Neither of us realized how much we needed help. The whole weekend was devoted to teaching married couples how to use a practical communication tool.

Most all married couples have ISSUES; topics that are surrounded by big neon signs saying, "Don't Even Think About Going There!" or "Touch This And You Die!" We had a few such issues at the time. They were like festering sores in the body of our relationship that hurt when we would touch them, so we intentionally avoided those issues. What we did not know was that they were steadily growing and dumping increasingly deadly toxins into the bloodstream of our marriage. The communication tool that we were taught proved to be a scalpel that we used to lance these sores, allowing the puss to be removed and a healing balm applied. It was a powerful weekend of healing for our marriage. If things had continued the way they were going before that weekend, our marriage could have been another casualty of the disease of hard-heartedness.

Married couples, who are having obvious problems, need to seek help NOW, if they wish their marriage to survive! Both parties need to humble themselves and be willing to take whatever steps necessary to restore health to their relationship before the toxin levels in the blood become critical and a terminal sickness takes hold. Once a terminal sickness takes hold, it can take a supernatural miracle of God to keep the marriage alive or resurrect it from the dead! The ultimate terminal sickness is hardening of the heart–a loss of all tenderness, compassion, love, and care for your spouse. In order for this to be fatal, only one partner need succumb to this deadly disease of the soul!

## WHY IS THERE SO MUCH DIVORCE TODAY?

There are many factors that have contributed to the dramatic increase in divorce that we have seen over the last half of a century. Some factors are obvious, like the general decay of morals in the American culture. Most movies and sitcoms today promote an immoral licentious lifestyle. Christian leadership and values are mocked and ridiculed on a regular basis. Pornography is not only available, but is constantly advertised through every form of media, especially the Internet. Today, a person must lead the life of a hermit in order not to be regularly bombarded by lustful and perverse images and concepts. Even billboards on the roadside promote all manner of filth and evil. Social constraints against divorce are now almost non-existent. The single parent home is no longer abnormal; and in some sectors of our society, it is the norm.

There are other factors that have led to an increase in divorce that are much subtler, like equal rights for women. Please do not misunderstand me, women should have equal rights; however, due to women no longer being as financially dependent upon their husbands as in years gone by, they no longer have to put up with as much abuse—rightly so. Also, women and men are now coworkers in almost every field. Often a person spends more time with a coworker than with his/her spouse. Temptation can be difficult to flee, especially if one's marriage is going through one of the many storms of life.

Another subtle, yet powerful factor in the increase in divorce is the tradition of dating. "Train up a child in the way he should go, and when he is old he will not depart from it" (Proverbs 22:6). Through dating, although they do not intend to get married any time soon, teenagers and even children are allowed, encouraged, and socially expected to have a girlfriend or boyfriend. They are taught to seek out and establish relationships based totally on their personal desires. As long as their "friend" fulfills these desires, the relationship continues. Once the child or teenager grows tired of the relationship, meets someone else that is more interesting or more attractive, or they move to another location or school, the relationship is terminated.

In platonic relationships, emotional and psychological ties are developed and then torn apart because of selfish reasons, developing in children and young adults, destructive relationship patterns and lifestyles. If they are sexually active, breaking up can be as psychologically, emotionally, physically, and as spiritually devastating as divorce, especially if the couple has had a child together.

Through dating, from childhood, children and young adults practice giving birth to and killing relationships. Why should we expect their marriages to be any different? We should teach our children how to establish, nurture, and maintain long-term healthy relationships.

Thankfully, principles of courting are being revived.[44] The primary principle of which is that exclusive relationships (boy/girl friend, "going steady," etc.) are not entered until a person is ready to marry. Who is ready to marry? Deciding this, a person must take into consideration one's age, financial stability, education level, housing, and career placement.

For people who are ready to get married, an interesting concept is the use of "match-making" services. These services help people broaden the pool of potential mates and identify others with a broad-based commonality. It is often said that opposites attract; however, in marriage, being the opposite gender is enough of a difference. In every other aspect of life, the more alike a couple is, the less conflict and greater potential for an enduring happy marriage. Above everything else, let us teach our children to seek the Lord for His wisdom, guidance and protection in every aspect of their lives, especially in spouse selection.

## What If Christians Divorce, May They Remarry?

Some Christians/churches attempt to draw a line between Christian and non-Christian divorcées, holding Christians to a "different" standard. Grace is shown non-Christian divorcées who are "allowed" to remarry because they divorced before they were in Christ. However, Christians who divorce are required not to remarry. Note that I did not say it was a "higher" standard, but a "different" one. It is not higher because it is based on error. Foremost, the Bible does not forbid any divorcées to marry again.

208 GOD IS A DIVORCÉ TOO!

Furthermore, towards whom does a father have more grace, his children or those who are not members of his family? It is a warped perspective of God to think that He has more grace and forgiveness for a non-believer than for one of His children! The good news for us all is that God loves us and our relationships with Him are based on His unconditional love and forgiveness, not upon our obedience to law. HALLELUJAH!

## WHAT ABOUT THE TEACHINGS OF THE CHURCH FATHERS?

While doing the research for this book, I came across an article that instigated an extended season of personal soul-searching, checking my motives and critiquing my beliefs. The article presented a convincing and compelling argument supporting the traditional doctrine of divorce. The author's argument was based on the teachings of the Church Fathers in the first few centuries after Christ. Prior to reading this article, I had never seriously considered the teachings of these men. This oversight on my part was predominantly due to my Evangelical heritage. Protestants and Evangelicals attempt to base their beliefs primarily, if not solely, upon the Bible. However, Roman Catholics have a much higher regard for the cumulative doctrine and traditions of the Church.

Hermas (AD 100–150) taught against divorce and remarriage, even if the wife was adulterous. If the man divorced his adulterous wife, he should remain single in the hopes that his wife will repent and return to him. Justin Martyr (AD 107–176) believed that remarriage after divorce was adultery. He even questioned whether or not a Christian woman, with an extremely immoral husband, should remain married and not divorce him. Athenagoras (AD 134–190), Tertullian (AD 160–211+), Clement of Alexandria (died AD 215), Basil of Caesarea (AD 329-379), John Chrysostom (AD 347-407), Ambrose (AD 374-397), Jerome (AD 340-420), and Augustine (AD 354-430), all held a hard-line when it came to divorce and remarriage. Divorce was forbidden except in the most extreme cases, even then it was considered questionable; and remarriage was always forbidden except for after the death of the ex-spouse.

If the Church Fathers held so tightly to the traditional doctrine of divorce, then who am I to disagree? These men lived in the Mediterranean area, physically much closer to Israel than I have ever visited. Considering the span of time that separates us from the days of Christ and the Apostles, these men are first cousins and I'm a distant relative. One must also take into consideration the unanimity with which they spoke–all denouncing divorce and remarriage. These are compelling reasons to give considerable weight to what they have written.

After prayerfully considering this information for several weeks, I came to the conclusion that we are in a pretty good position to challenge their stated beliefs. First of all, as a Protestant, I hold the Bible as the ultimate source of authority for all doctrine. If their beliefs disagree with what the Bible teaches, then I must disagree with their beliefs.

Secondly, we are brothers in Christ, not distant relatives. Through Christ and the Holy Spirit, we have access to God our Father just as much as they did at the time of their writings. Furthermore, due to the printing press and electronic communication tools that we have today, we have far greater access to the writings of the Apostles and other relevant material than they did.

Thirdly, and most importantly, concerning their living in the Mediterranean area in close proximity to Israel, due to their Greco-Roman heritage, they are actually more distant from Christ, culturally speaking, than many of us are today who have a Christian heritage. Concerning the Jewish culture from which Christ and the Apostles spoke, these men would have known much less than we know today, especially concerning the argument between the Shammaites and Hittites, and the original reason for the bill of divorce. Furthermore, as mentioned previously, Platonic and Stoic philosophy, Manichaeism, Gnosticism, and anti-Semitism would have significantly influenced these men.

Fourthly, another important thing to consider is the Church Fathers' promotion of celibacy as the preferable way to serve God. This culminated in the doctrine of priestly celibacy, which is also unscriptural. As was previously noted, the seeds of this overemphasis on celibacy are seen as early as the writing of I Corinthians. The Church Fathers also evidenced an unhealthy and unscriptural attitude towards marriage and sexual intimacy within marriage.

Fifthly, though they were united in their denouncement of divorce and remarriage, if their unanimity on this issue is based in corporate ignorance of the Jewish context concerning Jesus' words, and an undue exaltation of celibacy and dishonor of marriage, then their unanimity is not a serious concern.

Furthermore, to Protestants and Evangelicals it is compelling to note that the Puritans too rejected the traditional doctrine of divorce. John Milton, Puritan writer and theologian, author of Paradise Lost (AD 1608 – 1674) wrote two books concerning divorce, "The Doctrine and Discipline of Divorce I & II," which he gave to the English legislature in the hopes of persuading them to relax England's strict divorce laws. Milton argued that Jesus' difficult passages concerning divorce were overstatements, hyperbole, and not to be taken literally. He considered them exaggerations meant to rebuke the Pharisees. Milton further argued that they were not consistent with Jesus' other teachings or His office as a prophet. They were meant to speak to one's conscience, but not to be legislatively enforced in people's lives. Speaking of the traditional doctrine of divorce, Milton wrote:

> Our Saviours words touching divorce, are as it were congeal'd into a stony rigor, **inconsistent both with his doctrine and his office**; and that which he preacht onely to the conscience, is by **Canonicall tyranny** snatcht into the compulsive censure of a judiciall Court; where Laws are impos'd even against the venerable and secret power of natures impression, to love what ever cause be found to loath. **Which is a hainous barbarisme both against the honour of mariage, the dignity of man and his soule, the goodnes of Christianitie, and all the humane respects of civilitie.** (emphasis mine)[45]

If you can wade through the Old English, you will find that Milton's books on divorce are a rational and yet passionate plea for a dramatic change in the traditional doctrine of divorce and its legislation through civil government. He opposed the doctrine that marriage was a sacrament, under ecclesiastical authority, and indissoluble. He presented that marriage was a covenant, under civil authority, and breakable for a wide range of reasons, including irreconcilable differences! He endorsed that both parties of a divorce had a right of remarriage, regardless of the reasons for the divorce. Milton even went so far as to advocate removing divorce from public jurisdiction to private and not submitting couples seeking divorce to the shame of public divorce proceedings and scrutiny. He would likely have supported both the Any Matter divorce proceedings of Jesus' day, and the No Fault divorce proceedings of ours.

Should we blindly accept the teachings of the Church Fathers? No, they should be given significant weight in our deliberations, but ultimately we must rely most heavily upon scripture as our source of truth.

# Chapter XXI

# A DOCTRINE OF DEMONS

## DARLENE AND TROY

Darlene was happily married with three children when her world came apart; her husband divorced her for another woman. She found herself alone after twenty years of marriage. Not only did she lose her husband, but she also lost family and friends. Her in-laws were as emotionally close as her physical brothers and sisters; but they now had little, if any, contact with Darlene. Furthermore, almost all of her friends were married and were both she and her ex-husband's friends. There were no more couples-nights-out and she came to feel very awkward around these couples. Being around them seemed to magnify her loss and intensify her emotional pain.

Sadly, even Darlene's church abandoned her. Looking for companionship, Darlene stopped regularly attending church and began going places that her church did not condone. So they subjected her to official church discipline, breaking fellowship with her. They believed that this was the right and best thing to do; when what she really needed was a friend. It was terribly destructive for Darlene and her children. She was more alone, wounded, and broken than she had ever been in her life. Thoughts of suicide were her constant companion.

Thankfully, she soon found a good man who wanted to marry her. Even though Darlene's church had subjected her to church discipline, she still wanted to have a minister perform the wedding ceremony. Adding to her grief and stealing some of her joy, it proved to be difficult to find a willing minister because she and her fiancé were both divorcées. After a long and disheartening search, they found a retired minister and friend of the family that agreed to perform the ceremony.

Darlene, the good news is that God loves and cares for you. He felt your pain, carried you through the rejection and loss of your husband, family, friends, and church, and is with you today. God understands your pain having experienced rejection, loss, and even divorce, Himself. He not only recognizes your current marriage, but has blessed you and your family with a good man, your new husband, Troy. Love him with all of your heart and let the pain of the past and the unfulfilled dreams of your previous marriage be washed away in the river of His love. May you and your loved ones be filled with the abundant life of Christ! He is The Comforter.

The traditional doctrine of divorce is fatally flawed at a conceptual level. It is based on false premises and subtle, but tragic misinterpretations of scripture; and is diametrically opposed to God's grace, forgiveness, and original design of mankind! In I Timothy 4:1-3 the Bible says,

> *Now the Spirit expressly says that in latter times some will depart from the faith, giving heed to deceiving spirits and **doctrines of demons**, speaking lies in hypocrisy, having their own conscience seared with a hot iron, **forbidding to marry** (NKJV).*

As an Evangelical Protestant, I have always read this passage thinking of the Catholic doctrine of priestly celibacy, but the traditional doctrine of divorce also forbids people to marry—the divorcée. Could it be that the traditional doctrine of divorce is a doctrine of demons birthed by deceiving spirits? Absolutely! Deceiving spirits are evil spirits that influence people in such a way as to have us accept lies as the truth. These lies then form the foundation for doctrine and the way that we live. A doctrine that is based on such lies is a doctrine of demons.

The traditional doctrine of divorce is like a spider's web, being made up of multiple interconnected strands of lies. Each strand is a false belief or misinterpretation of scripture. These small and seemingly insignificant strands overlap, reinforcing each other, and making the web a formidable trap to an unsuspecting bird. Like a spider, Satan has spun this web of deceit in the hopes of slowly killing those he might capture in its grip, sucking out their lifeblood—the love, forgiveness, joy, hope, and peace found in Christ. Some people are so tightly wrapped in this web that they can move neither forward or back, and fearfully anticipate their doom having no hope of escape. Tragically, it is a slow and agonizing death that they are sure to receive, *unless they are delivered.*

Let us briefly review the major errors, the predominant lies, which are the foundation of the traditional doctrine of divorce:

## Lie #1
**Marriage is a Sacrament.**

## Truth #1
**Marriage is NOT a Sacrament**

Marriage is a covenant-based relationship whereby a man and woman are legally and socially yoked together for the purpose of establishing a new family. Baptism and the Eucharist are good examples of sacraments. A sacrament is something administered in and by the church for believers. Marriage is not for believers only; it is for all of mankind and therefore needs to be governed in a manner that applies to all people, and not just believers. For Christian married couples, it is healthy and appropriate to understand their marital relationships as sacred and holy before God. However, claiming marriage to be a sacrament only lead to other even more grievous errors.

## Lie #2
**Marriage is under
Ecclesiastical authority.**

## Truth #2
**Marriage is under
Civil authority.**

Marriage is under civil authority and not ecclesiastical authority. Although Christian leaders might act and speak like the church has such authority, it clearly does not. Please note that I am not saying that issues concerning marriage and divorce are not under God's authority, but that they are not under the church's authority. God has delegated such authority to civil governments and will hold civic leaders accountable for the manner in which they administer this authority, good or evil. Similar to laws concerning abuse, neglect, theft, or murder, marriage and divorce are under civil authority. Apart from delegated civil authority, ministers do not have the authority to declare who is married and who is not, in the eyes of man or God.

## Lie #3
**Marriage is indissoluble.**

## Truth #3
**Marriage is NOT indissoluble.**

Marriage is breakable and should be understood and treated as such. Death or a legal divorce breaks the marriage bond. If a married couple divorces, legally breaking their marriage, regardless of the reason, the marital union no longer exists on earth or in heaven! As Martin Luther said, *"Marriage is a very worldly thing."* Jesus commands to not divorce because divorce is possible, not because divorce is impossible.

## Lie #4
**Moses was in error when he instituted the bill of divorce.**

## Truth #4
**Moses was fully inspired by God in establishing the bill of divorce.**

Moses was inspired by God to establish civil and religious laws and authority structures for the nation of Israel. In doing so, he was specific about guidelines concerning marriage, divorce, and remarriage. Moses placed marriage under civil authority (the city leaders). He recognized that marriage is breakable and that married couples separate, so he endorsed the giving of a bill of divorce in order to protect women from being relegated to a life of adultery. Moses did not establish (or attempt to establish) acceptable or non-acceptable reasons for divorce. Such matters were governed primarily by the common Near Eastern practice of the guilty party being penalized financially for the divorce.

## Lie #5
**Jesus wished to repudiate
the bill of divorce.**

## Truth #5
**Jesus endorsed
the bill of divorce.**

Jesus explicitly stated that not one word of the Law would be changed, assuming the full inspiration of the Mosaic Law including the bill of divorce. There is no scriptural precedence to suggest that Jesus intended to change the Law of Moses concerning divorce; nor did He intend to give "teeth to the Law," making it stricter. Jesus did not condemn divorcées. He did not say or imply that a divorced person should remain celibate. Jesus elevated women to an equal standing with men by holding men accountable for adultery for those who were unfaithful to their wives in thought or deed. He underscored marriage as a work of God, something God has a vital interest in, and affirmed the divine ideal of marriage as a monogamous, exclusive union of a man and woman in an interdependent family relationship.

## Lie #6
**Jesus legislated adultery
as the only acceptable
reason for divorce.**

## Truth #6
**Jesus did NOT legislate
acceptable or non-acceptable
reasons for divorce.**

Jesus spoke as a prophet and not as a legislator. He recognized the need for civil legal divorce proceedings, but did not attempt to legislate a specific philosophy or procedure other than endorsing the Mosaic bill of divorce. Jesus also assumed that divorce would continue because of the hardness of heart in mankind. Jesus' words concerning marriage and divorce do not support the traditional doctrine of divorce.

## Lie #7

**Paul legislated another acceptable reason for divorce other than adultery.**

## Truth #7

**Paul did NOT legislate either acceptable or non-acceptable reasons for divorce.**

The Apostle Paul understood that people are responsible before God to make their own decisions concerning their marriages. He therefore empowered his children in the faith to make the best decisions considering their individual circumstances. He also gave a practical example of weighing applicable principles of God concerning marriages in crisis.

## Lie #8

**God hates divorce.**

## Truth #8

**God does NOT hate divorce.**

God hates the sin that leads to divorce, but inspired Moses to institute the bill of divorce to free abandoned women to remarry legally and remain married. The scripture in Malachi 2:16 condemns the practice of the "hateful divorce," a divorce based on selfish reasons, and particularly divorces based on the desire to marry someone else.

## Lie #9

**Divorcés must not remarry.**

## Truth #9

**Divorcés may remarry.**

The Bible specifically says that a divorcé that marries again does not sin! What a tremendous contradiction to the traditional doctrine of divorce!

## Lie #10

**There are scriptural and non-scriptural reasons for divorce.**

## Truth #10

**There are NOT scriptural and non-scriptural reasons for divorce.**

The Bible does not legislate acceptable or non-acceptable reasons for divorce. However, there are moral and immoral reasons for divorce, but only God knows the motives of one's heart. We are responsible before God concerning our marriages to make our own decisions based on biblical principles and our individual circumstances. We need not allow minister, priest, or self-appointed hypocritical judge to bring us under religious bondage in these regards.

The traditional doctrine of divorce is based upon errors and misinterpretations of scripture. Divorce is neither right nor wrong; it just *is!* Depending on a myriad of personal factors and the personal application of biblical principles, divorce can be the right thing to do. Let me restate that; <u>in some cases, divorce can be the right thing and the best thing to do</u>. Even God, motivated by His love for Israel, divorced her (Jeremiah 3:8).

Divorce can also be the absolute worst thing to do and usually is. Married couples can make it through any storm, even the level five hurricane of adultery, if they will only allow God to soften their hearts towards each other and repent of their selfishness.

## The Church's Responsibility

⊙ Our first priority is *to assist individuals in growing* in the Christ-like character of sacrificial love–discipleship. Sacrificial love is the foundation for enduring relationships.

⊙ We should *support married couples in building an "ideal" marriage*— a faithful and loving union of a man and woman in a healthy interdependent family relationship.

⊙ Through prayer and civic action, we should *support government in establishing and enforcing laws* that protect children, that punish abusive or negligent spouses, and that facilitate the empowerment of marriages and the restoration of those in crisis.

⊙ We should *provide communities of acceptance that promote the healing of individuals and families* that have experienced the ravages of divorce.

⊙ With one hand we *must hold tightly to Jesus*; with the other hand we must *reach out and embrace broken humanity.*

Where there is strife, we should sow peace. Where there is hate, we should sow love. Where there is despair, we should sow hope. Where there has been condemnation and rejection, we should sow forgiveness and acceptance!

If someone's Kabluck, marriage bull (mentioned in Chapter 3) is about to be killed, we should do all that we can to save it. If the Kabluck has been killed, we should help free those that are chained to pieces of its rotting flesh. Jesus came to set captives free; to heal the broken hearted, and to help people find and travel the trail of hope through the valley of despair! As the body of Christ, we should do the same.

We need the Spirit of God in these days of rampant divorce. We need to be filled with the Spirit of wisdom and understanding, the Spirit of counsel and might, the Spirit of knowledge and the fear of the Lord! (Isaiah 11:2) Only Jesus can heal the broken hearted. Only Jesus can raise the dead to life and heal the hardness of our hearts. Only Jesus can restore our broken relationships.

If you are contemplating divorce, please exhaust every means of prayer, counsel, ministry, and deliverance before taking that fateful step. If you are in an adulterous relationship (thought or deed), flee that relationship like a bat-out-of-hell! Change jobs! Move out of town! Make radical changes doing whatever it takes to protect your marriage! Guard it like Fort Knox, for it is valuable and fragile!

If you are living together without being legally married, for your sake and the sake of all those whom you love, especially your children, please either marry or go your separate ways. Establishing a legal covenant of marriage is a defining point in any relationship. Are you committed to this person and his/her welfare, or not?

## REASONS TO BE LEGALLY WED

⊙ Sexual intimacy outside of marriage is wrong. It is sinful and cannot help but bring death and destruction to you and your loved ones, regardless of how wonderful and fulfilling it might feel.

⊙ True emotional health—consistent feelings of love, joy, and peace can only grow and mature in the fertile seedbed of covenant relationships.

⊙ Spiritually, marriage honors God as opposed to living together, which dishonors Him; and you do not want to do that! The fear of God, is the beginning of wisdom (Proverbs 9:10).

⊙ Marriage honors your parents and other family members, as opposed to living together which shames them; and honoring your parents is the first of the Ten Commandments with a promise of a blessing from God. If you would see long life and good days, honor your parents.

⊙ Finally, if you wish for God to be personally involved in helping you stay together as a couple, allow Him to join you together as husband and wife through a legal covenant of marriage!

Women, please do not let a man deceive you into living or continuing to live with him like a wife without the protection and honor of marriage. As a general rule, men are not nearly as sensitive as women, and do not feel the need as strongly as women do for the emotional, social, and financial security provided by marriage. Therefore do not allow a man to take advantage of you in such a way.

Men, do not even claim to love the woman that you are living with unless you will marry her! Love demands that you place her wellbeing (emotional, psychological, social, and spiritual) above your own selfish desires or fears.

Several years ago the Holy Spirit explained something to me as I prayerfully considered I Peter 3:7:

*Husbands, likewise, dwell with them with understanding, giving honor to the wife, as to the weaker vessel, and as being heirs together of the grace of life, that your prayers may not be hindered* (NKJV).

In prayer I asked God, "What do you mean by this? Chantal (*my wife*) is a strong woman. She's intelligent and has a stronger, more forceful personality than me. What do you mean by she's the 'weaker vessel?'"

If you've ever heard God speak to you, His few words communicate volumes. God spoke to me saying, "*I made you like a cast-iron pot, but Chantal is like a China vase.*" I understood that I needed to treat Chantal with great gentleness. One does not handle an expensive China vase like he would a cast-iron pot. She is delicate and of unimaginable worth and needs to be handled as such.

I have also heard it said that, "*If words are like pebbles and men are like buffaloes, then women are like butterflies.*" You may drop a ton of pebbles (harsh words) on a buffalo and he will shake them off and keep on grazing! However, a single pebble (harsh word) has the potential of injuring a butterfly so that it never flies again. Men, we have been given an awesome responsibility and privilege in caring for our wives and children. May God help us make gentleness, kindness, and patience a vital part of who we are and how we relate to them!

> *Love is kind and patient, never jealous, boastful, proud, or rude.*
> *Love isn't selfish or quick-tempered.*
> *Love doesn't keep a record of wrongs that others do.*
> *Love rejoices in the truth, but not in evil.*
> *Love is always supportive, loyal, hopeful, and trusting.*
> *Love never fails!* (I Corinthians 13:4-8a)

The good news for the divorcée is that God loves you with an everlasting love. *Divorce is not the unforgivable sin!* God understands your pain, having experienced it himself. Yes, God is a divorcé too! The Comforter, the Holy Spirit, has been given to us so that every broken heart might be healed by His love. Embrace Jesus with all of your heart and He will give you abundant life!

If you take a $100 bill and soak it in mud and rip it into little pieces, how much is it worth? $100 of course! In the same way, no matter how much filth we have soaked in or how broken we have become, we are still of unimaginable value and worth to God, just like a newborn baby. God has provided a means of cleansing and restoration for us all—the blood of Jesus Christ through His sacrificial death on the cross. "*God so loved the world, that He gave His one and only Son, that whosoever believes in Him will not perish, but will have everlasting life*" (John 3:16).

If you have never allowed Jesus to cleanse you from the filth of this world, ask Him and He will. In the final analysis, Jesus is the only one that can fill the loneliness inside each of us. Only through Jesus can we truly have healthy interdependent relationships, dining from the same bowl of eternal-life cereal. That statement is a little corny; and I hope that it made you smile, but even more so, I pray that you will be filled with the love and life that is found only in Jesus!

If you have never received Jesus as your Lord and Savior, today He is knocking at the door of your heart asking to come in and live with you. He is a gentleman and will not force His way in; He must be invited. Invite Jesus into your heart and you too will have eternal life!

*The Lord God said, 'It is not good for the man to be alone. I will make a helper suitable for him'* (Genesis 2:18 NIV).

The divine ideal of marriage is a monogamous, faithful, life-long union of a man and woman in a healthy, interdependent, familial relationship. We need to do all we can to help this become a reality in people's lives; but divorce happens, so we, the church, must learn to deal with it based in truth, grace, and mercy.

Divorce is usually devastating, resulting in long-term negative emotional, psychological, financial, spiritual, and even physical problems. For many, especially the children of divorce, it can be like being chained to a piece of dead rotting flesh, fostering death and disease for years, even generations to come. Those who have or are going through divorce do not need our social or religious judgement, condemnation, or punishment; the natural ramifications of their actions are punishment enough! If punishment in such domestic matters is needed, it is the responsibility of the civil government to do so, not the church. Divorcées need our prayers and support. In order to be able to give such support, we must walk in humility, realizing that but for the grace of God, "there go I," always remembering that God is a divorcé too!

# SCRIPTURE INDEX

# BIBLIOGRAPHY

*A Greek-English Lexicon of the New Testament and Other Early Christian Literature, Second Edition.* Chicago and London: University of Chicago Press, 1979.

Barna, George. *The Future of the American Family.* Chicago: Moody Press, 1993.

*Beacon Dictionary of Theology.* Kansas City, Missouri: Beacon Hill Press, 1983. Richard S. Taylor, editor.

Cloud, Drs. Henry and John Townsend. *Boundaries: Gaining Control of Your Life.* Grand Rapids, MI: Zondervan, 1992.

Cloud, Drs. Henry and John Townsend. *Boundaries in Marriage.* Grand Rapids, MI: Zondervan, 1999.

Davis, John Jefferson. *Evangelical Ethics: Issues Facing The Church Today.* Phillipsburg, New Jersey: Presbyterian And Reformed Publishing Co., 1985.

*Encyclopedia of the Early Church.* New York: Oxford University Press, 1992.

Grunlan, Stephen A. *Marriage and the Family: A Christian Perspective.* Grand Rapids, Michigan: Academie Books, 1984.

Harris, Joshua. *I Kissed Dating Goodbye.* Sisters, Oregon: Multnomah Publishers Inc., 1997.

Hayford, Jack. *Newborn: Your New Life In Christ.* Wheaton, Illinois: Tyndale House Publishers Inc., 1971.

Howard, George Elliot. *"Divorce."* In New Schaff-Herzog Religious Encyclopedia, ed. S.M. Case. New York: Funk and Wagnalls, 1909.

Hugenberger, G. P. *Marriage as a Covenant: Biblical Law and Ethics as Developed from Malachi.* Vetus Testamentum Supplement 52. Leiden and New York: Brill, 1994.

Hurtado, Larry W. *Mark, A Good News Commentary*. San Francisco: Harper and Row Publishers, 1966.

Instone-Brewer, David. *Divorce And Remarriage in the Bible: The Social and Literary Context.* Grand Rapids, Michigan: William B. Eerdmans Publishing Co. 2002.

Lamsa, George M. *Gospel Light: Comments of the Teachings of Jesus from Aramaic and Unchanged Eastern Customs.* Philadelphia: A. J. Holman Company, 1936.

Lane, William L. *The Gospel According To Mark*. In The New International Commentary On The New Testament. Grand Rapids, Michigan: William B. Eerdmans Publishing Co., 1974.

Milton, John. *The Doctrine and Discipline of Divorce*. Originally addressed to the English Parliament and the Westminster Assembly of Divines in 1643. View via the Internet Resources of Dartmouth College, Hanover, NH. www.dartmouth.edu/~milton/reading_room/ddd/book_1/index.shtml

*New Catholic Encyclopedia*. San Francisco: The Catholic University of America, 1964.

*Noah Webster's First Edition of an American Dictionary of the English Language*. Foundation for American Christian Education, San Francisco, CA, 1995. Reprint of the 1828 edition.

Parker, David. *The Early Traditions of Jesus' Sayings on Divorce*. In Theology, September/October, 1993. London: SCM Press LTD.

Ryken, Leland. *Worldly Saints: The Puritans as they Really Were*. Grand Rapids, Michigan: Academie Books, 1986.

Story, Cullen IK & J. Lyle Story. *Greek To Me*. San Francisco: HarperCollins Publishers, 1979.

Strong, James. *New Strong's Dictionary of Hebrew and Greek Words*. electronic ed., Logos Library System. Nashville: Thomas Nelson, 1997.

Von Buseck, Craig. *Seven Keys to Hearing God's Voice*. Tulsa, Oklahoma: Hensley Publishing, 2004.

*Webster's New Collegiate Dictionary.* Springfield, Massachusetts: G. & C. Merriam Co., 1981.

Westbrook, Raymond. *Prohibition of Restoration of Marriage in Deuteronomy 24:1-4.* In *Studies in Bible* 1986 ed. S. Japhet, pp. 387-405. Scripta Hierosolymitana 31. Jerusalem: Magnes, 1986.

*World Book Encyclopedia.* Chicago: World Book, Inc., 1990.

# (ENDNOTES)

1 "Divorce." New Catholic Encyclopedia." 2: 928.
2 The Pauline Privilege as stated in I Corinthians 7:15 "If your husband or wife isn't a follower of the Lord and decides to divorce you, then you should agree to it. You are no longer bound to that person."
3 "Marriage." *Webster's New Collegiate Dictionary.* 698.
4 "Marriage." *American Dictionary of the English Language,* Noah Webster 1828.
5 Jack Hayford. *Newborn, Your New Life In Christ.* 36-38.
6 "Marry." *Webster's New Collegiate Dictionary.* 699.
7 David Instone-Brewer. *Divorce and Remarriage in the Bible.* 19.
8 "Common Law Marriage." *Webster's New Collegiate Dictionary.* 225.
9 Story author unknown, received via email.
10 "Divorce." *American Dictionary of the English Language,* Noah Webster 1828.
11 "Plato." *World Book Encyclopedia.* 15: 570.
12 "Sacrament." *Webster's New Collegiate Dictionary.* 1009.
13 David Instone-Brewer. *Divorce and Remarriage in the Bible.* 255-256.
14 "μυστήριον." *A Greek-English Lexicon of the New Testament.* 530.
15 George Elliot Howard. "Divorce." *New Schaff-Herzog Religious Encyclopedia.* 3:454.
16 "Marriage." *Encyclopedia of the Early Church.* 529.
17 Leland Ryken, *Worldly Saints: The Puritans as they Really Were.*
18 Josephus. *The Antiquities of the Jews.* book 18, chapter 5, verse 136.
19 "Indissoluble." *Webster's New Collegiate Dictionary.* 1009.
20 John Jefferson Davis. *Evangelical Ethics: Issues Facing The Church Today.* 93.
21 Dr. David Instone-Brewer. *Divorce and Remarriage in the Bible.* 21-22.
22 Ibid., 6.
23 Ibid., 28-33.
24 Ibid., 30.
25 "Divorce." *New Catholic Encyclopedia.* 2: 929.
26 David Parker. *The Early Traditions of Jesus' Sayings on Divorce.* 379-380.
27 "Legalism", *Beacon Dictionary of Theology,* 311.
28 David Instone-Brewer, *Divorce and Remarriage in the Bible.* 133-136.
29 Ibid., 93.
30 Ibid., 111.
31 Ibid., 110-114.
32 "**Apŏluo**," *New Strong's Dictionary of Hebrew and Greek Words, electronic ed., Logos Library System.*

[33] Lane, William L. *The Gospel According To Mark.* 358.
[34] George M. Lamsa. *Gospel Light.* 38.
[35] Larry W. Hurtado, *Mark. A Good News Commentary.* 154.
[36] Cullen IK Story & J. Lyle Story. *Greek To Me.* 194.
[37] David Instone-Brewer, *Divorce and Remarriage in the Bible.* 159.
[38] William L. Lane. *The Gospel According To Mark.* 357.
[39] David Instone-Brewer, *Divorce and Remarriage in the Bible.* 227.
[40] Gordon P. Hugenberger, *Marriage as a Covenant.* v. 14 - p. 27, v. 15 - p. 126, v. 16 - p. 76.
[41] Raymond Westbrook, *Prohibition of Restoration of Marriage in Deuteronomy 24:1-4.*
[42] David Instone-Brewer, *Divorce and Remarriage in the Bible.* 56-57.
[43] "Justify." *Webster's New Collegiate Dictionary.* 623.
[44] A good book on courting is *I Kissed Dating Goodbye* by Joshua Harris.
[45] John Milton, *The Doctrine and Discipline of Divorce*, Preface to Book I.

Contact Sherman Nobles
www.ShermanNobles.com
or order more copies of this book at


TATE PUBLISHING, LLC


127 East Trade Center Terrace
Mustang, Oklahoma 73064

(888) 361-9473

Tate Publishing, LLC


www.tatepublishing.com